OH MY, NELLIE BLY

Book by Nick Stimson

Music and Lyrics by
Annemarie Lewis Thomas

samuelfrench.co.uk

Copyright © 2018 by Annemarie Lewis Thomas (lyrics and music)
and Nick Stimson (book) and All Rights Reserved

OH MY, NELLIE BLY is fully protected under the copyright laws of the British Commonwealth, including Canada, the United States of America, and all other countries of the Copyright Union. All rights, including professional and amateur stage productions, recitation, lecturing, public reading, motion picture, radio broadcasting, television and the rights of translation into foreign languages are strictly reserved.

ISBN 978-0-573-11636-0
www.samuelfrench.co.uk
www.samuelfrench.com

Cover design by ©Daniel Evans

For Professional and Amateur Production Enquiries

United Kingdom and World excluding North America
plays@samuelfrench.co.uk
020 7255 4302/01

United States and Canada
info@samuelfrench.com
020 7255 4302/01

Each title is subject to availability from Samuel French, depending upon country of performance.

CAUTION: Professional and amateur producers are hereby warned that *OH MY, NELLIE BLY* is subject to a licensing fee. Publication of this play does not imply availability for performance. Both amateurs and professionals considering a production are strongly advised to apply to the appropriate agent before starting rehearsals, advertising, or booking a theatre. A licensing fee must be paid whether the title is presented for charity or gain and whether or not admission is charged.

The professional rights in this play are controlled by Janet Fillingham Associates, 52 Lowther Road, London SW13 9NU.

No one shall make any changes in this title for the purpose of production. No part of this book may be reproduced, stored in a retrieval system, or transmitted in any form, by any means, now known or yet to be invented, including mechanical, electronic, photocopying, recording, videotaping, or otherwise, without the prior written permission of the publisher. No one shall upload this title, or part of this title, to any social media websites.

The right of Annemarie Lewis Thomas to be identified as composer and lyricist and Nick Stimson to be identified as author of this work has been asserted in accordance with Section 77 of the Copyright, Designs and Patents Act 1988.

THINKING ABOUT PERFORMING A SHOW?

There are thousands of plays and musicals available to perform from Samuel French right now, and applying for a licence is easier and more affordable than you might think

From classic plays to brand new musicals, from monologues to epic dramas, there are shows for everyone.

Plays and musicals are protected by copyright law, so if you want to perform them, the first thing you'll need is a licence. This simple process helps support the playwright by ensuring they get paid for their work and means that you'll have the documents you need to stage the show in public.

Not all our shows are available to perform all the time, so it's important to check and apply for a licence before you start rehearsals or commit to doing the show.

LEARN MORE & FIND THOUSANDS OF SHOWS

Browse our full range of plays and musicals, and find out more about how to license a show
www.samuelfrench.co.uk/perform

Talk to the friendly experts in our Licensing team for advice on choosing a show and help with licensing
plays@samuelfrench.co.uk   020 7387 9373

Acting Editions
BORN TO PERFORM

Playscripts designed from the ground up to work the way you do in rehearsal, performance and study

---

Larger, clearer text for easier reading

Wider margins for notes

Performance features such as character and props lists, sound and lighting cues, and more

---

+ CHOOSE A SIZE AND STYLE TO SUIT YOU

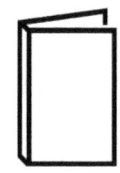  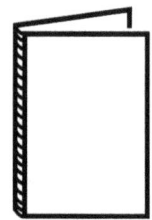

STANDARD EDITION
Our regular paperback book at our regular size

SPIRAL-BOUND EDITION
The same size as the Standard Edition, but with a sturdy, easy-to-fold, easy-to-hold spiral-bound spine

LARGE EDITION
A4 size and spiral bound, with larger text and a blank page for notes opposite every page of text – perfect for technical and directing use

---

| LEARN MORE | samuelfrench.co.uk/actingeditions

Other musicals by NICK STIMSON and ANNEMARIE LEWIS THOMAS published and licensed by Samuel French

Around the World in Eighty Days with book and lyrics by Phil Willmott

Dangerous Daughters

FIND PERFECT PLAYS TO PERFORM AT
www.samuelfrench.co.uk/perform

ABOUT THE COMPOSER AND LYRICIST

Annemarie Lewis Thomas

Annemarie Lewis Thomas is a composer, lyricist and an accomplished musical director and arranger.

Full-length musicals include: in collaboration with Phil Willmott, Annemarie wrote the music to *Around the World in Eighty Days*, *Uncle Ebenezer* and *The Wolf Boys*. In collaboration with Gerry Flanagan, Annemarie wrote the music and lyrics to *Great Expectations* and *Fool's Gold*. Other shows with Nick Stimson include *The Sunshine Gang*, *The Ballad of Kitty Jay*, *Just the Ticket*, *Celebs Anon* and *The Venus Factor*.

In collaboration with Daniel O'Brien she has written the original songs for seven pantomimes, three of which were commissioned for the Theatre Royal, Bury St Edmunds.

As the MD for the award-winning Steam Industry, Annemarie worked on all of the critically acclaimed BAC Christmas musicals. Other credits include: *Rent* (Olympia Theatre, Dublin), *Annie* (UK No 1 Tour), UK premieres *Victor/Victoria*, *Reefer Madness* (Bridewell), *Naked Boys Singing* (Madam Jojo's), *Martin Charnin's 9 and a Half Quid Revue 9* (the King's Head).

In 2009 Annemarie opened The MTA (The Musical Theatre Academy), running the UK's first accelerated learning programme for performers. It was named as the School of the Year in The Stage 100 Awards in 2012 and 2017.

ABOUT THE AUTHOR

Nick Stimson

Nick Stimson is a freelance playwright, theatre director and poet. He is also Associate Director of the Theatre Royal, Plymouth. Productions include: writer of *A Winter's Tale* (with the composer Howard Goodall) at The Sage, Gateshead and the Yvonne Arnaud Theatre, Guildford and Landor Theatre, London (winner of Best Off West musical at the Offies 2014); *Sailors and Sweethearts*, a play about the artist Beryl Cook, at the Drum Theatre, Plymouth; writer and director of *NHS The Musical* (with music by Jimmy Jewell) at the Drum Theatre, Plymouth and the The Venue, Leicester Square, London; writer of *Hello Mister Capello* for the Palace Theatre, Watford; co-writer of *Promised Land* (written with Anthony Clavane) for Red Ladder Theatre, the Carriage Works, Leeds; writer of *Who Ate All the Pies?* (with music by Jimmy Jewell) at the Tristan Bates Theatre, London; writer of *The Venus Factor* and *The Sunshine Gang* (with music and lyrics by Annemarie Lewis Thomas) for the MTA at the Bridewell Theatre, London; writer and director of *Korczak* (with music by Chris Williams) at Theatre Royal, Plymouth, YMTUK at The Rose Theatre, London and Bialystok Opera Poland (international tour); writer and director of *The Day We Played Brazil* (with music by Chris Williams) for the Northcott Theatre, Exeter; writer of *Inventing Utopia* a play about Dorothy and Leonard Elmhirst, for production at Dartington; co-writer (with Anthony Clavane) of *Leeds Lads* for Red Ladder Theatre at the Carriage Works, Leeds.

AUTHOR'S NOTE

Oh My, Nellie Bly is the often comic and sometimes tragic story of the adventures of the USA's first female journalist. Nellie became internationally renowned for her daring and outrageous journalistic stunts. She got herself committed to New York's infamous insane asylum on Blackwell's Island in order to expose the cruelties of the regime. She made a solo journey around the world to better the eighty days taken in Jules Verne's famous novel. A complex and driven character, she sacrificed personal happiness and love to be first to the story.

The framework of the musical is Nellie's spectacular 1889 solo journey around the world. Nellie is accompanied on her journey by the Gibson Girl, a figment of Nellie's imagination brought to life through Nellie's deep-seated loneliness and insecurity. (The Gibson Girl was a contemporary cartoon character epitomising the go-ahead super-confident ideal of the American womanhood.) In France Nellie meets Jules Verne and his beautiful wife Honorine. On a steamer going from Italy to Egypt Nellie turns down three proposals of marriage. In Hong Kong Nellie shocks the refined ladies of the British Empire when she learns she has a rival, another female journalist, also attempting a solo journey around the world.

When Nellie reaches China on Christmas Day 1889 she loses her self-belief. The Gibson Girl takes Nellie back to the Insane Asylum where Nellie relives the terrible experiences she endured there.

Confident once again, Nellie returns to her journey and the trip around the world in just seventy-two days. At the moment of her greatest triumph she turns to share her victory with the Gibson Girl, but the Gibson Girl has vanished.

Nick Stimson & Annemarie Lewis Thomas

MUSIC USE NOTE

Licensees are solely responsible for obtaining formal written permission from copyright owners to use copyrighted music in the performance of this play and are strongly cautioned to do so. If no such permission is obtained by the licensee, then the licensee must use only original music that the licensee owns and controls. Licensees are solely responsible and liable for all music clearances and shall indemnify the copyright owners of the play(s) and their licensing agent, Samuel French, against any costs, expenses, losses and liabilities arising from the use of music by licensees. Please contact the appropriate music licensing authority in your territory for the rights to any incidental music.

IMPORTANT BILLING AND CREDIT REQUIREMENTS

If you have obtained performance rights to this title, please refer to your licensing agreement for important billing and credit requirements.

We would like to thank:

Simon Kane, Chris Whittaker, Stewart J. Charlesworth, Jon Varley, George Bach, Aylin Altinelli, Amy Pickard, Lesley McNamara, Lucy Fowler, Antonia Petrucelli, Elizabeth Gethings, Laura Thatcher, Daniel Evans, Mat Elliott, Paul Merser, Calyssa Davidson and Jack Pennifold for making the original production so special. We would also like to thank our agent Kate Weston at Janet Fillingham Associates for believing in this show and thanks also to Derek Stubbs for his French language expertise.

Annemarie would like to dedicate this show to Angie, Adrian & Alfie, and to the amazing woman that taught her that anything was possible if you wanted to do it – her mum.

Nick would like to dedicate this show to the up and coming stars of the future: Joe, Charlie, Otis, Eddie, Arlo and Wilbur.

The MTA & Mental Health.

The MTA is a multi-award winning musical theatre college, recognised as being one of the most forward-thinking drama colleges in the UK when it comes to mental health. In 2016, it initiated the industry-wide #time4change Mental Health Charter. Whilst this piece acknowledges the difference made by Nellie Bly by highlighting the mistreatment that was taking place in the Blackwell Island Asylum, we also recognise that society as a whole still has a long way to go to see mental illness in the same way as we see physical illness.

A percentage of all royalties from this show will go directly to The MTA's Student Hardship Fund.

FIRST PERFORMANCE INFO

Oh My, Nellie Bly was commissioned by The MTA. It's first production was on 12 September 2018 at the Bridewell Theatre, London. The original cast were all first years on The MTA's two-year Musical Theatre Diploma.

Amber Whitehouse – Honorine / Mrs Murray-McMurray
Andrea Mizzen – Guard / Miss Blower-Blower-Fitzroy
Eleanor Lewis – Gibson Girl
Ella Rusbridger – Mrs Anstruther / Inmate / Leper
Emma Maywood – Catherine / Miss Selhurst-Winner
Georgina-mae Hall – Elizabeth Bisland / Lady Ponsonby-Breedlove-Godalming
Joséphine Castadot – Anna (Inmate) / Miss Jones
Jacob Swann – Jules Verne / Curzon / Thomas/ Giovanni / Captain Smith / Dr Kinier
Laura Gómez Gracia – Interpreter / Aileen (Inmate)
Mara Nunes – Miss Needham / Miss McCarten
Maria Karélina – Tillie Maynard
Rafaela Seipião – Sarah (Inmate) / Leper / 1st American Woman
Rosie Riley-Best – Miss Fordham-Buller / Leper / 2nd American Woman
Samantha Hedley – Miss Grupe
Sarah Hjort – Mary Hughes (Inmate) / Leper / Miss Whickerton-Snickerton
Tatiana Chater Davies – Nellie Bly
Ursula Earley – Mrs Cochran

CHARACTERS

16+ Female 1–8 Male (Doubling possible)

WOMEN

NELLIE BLY – Tomboyish, confident, perky and highly ambitious young woman. Underlying deep-rooted fear of failure.

THE GIBSON GIRL – A popular cartoon character created by Charles Dana Gibson from *Scribner's Magazine*. The epitome of the modern American young woman of the late nineteeth century. Great self-belief and in charge of her own destiny.

CATHERINE COCHRAN – NELLIE's younger sister. Tomboyish and happy-go-lucky but lacks NELLIE's driving ambition.

MRS COCHRAN – NELLIE and CATHERINE's widowed mother. Conservative and old-fashioned.

HONORINE VERNE – The French wife of the novelist JULES VERNE. Lives in her husband's shadow. Elegant, sensitive and intelligent.

INTERPRETER – Cold and haughty. Doing her job.

MRS ANSTRUTHER – Wife of an official in British Hong Kong.

MISS FORDHAM-BULLER – Wife of an official in British Hong Kong.

MRS MCURRAY-MCMURRAY – Wife of an official in British Hong Kong.

MRS BLOWER-BLOWER-FITZROY – Wife of an official in British Hong Kong.

MRS PONSONBY-BREEDLOVE-GODALMING – Wife of a General in British Hong Kong.

MISS WHICKERTON-SNICKERTON – Wife of an official in British Hong Kong.

MISS FELICITY SELHURST-WINNER – Wife of an official in British Hong Kong

ELIZABETH BISLAND – NELLIE's rival in the great race around the world. A young journalist. More conservative than NELLIE. Not enjoying her solo trip around the world.

MISS GRUPE – Cruel, crude and violent nurse in the insane asylum.

TILLIE MAYNARD – An inmate in the insane asylum. Lost, confused and frightened.

MARY HUGHES – An inmate in the insane asylum. Pines for her children.

MISS MCCARTEN – A flirtatious and uncaring nurse in the insane asylum.

SARAH – A violent inmate in the insane asylum.

ANNA – An inmate in the insane asylum. Convinced her mother is coming to rescue her.

CLARA – An inmate in the insane asylum who believes she is damned for all eternity.

AILEEN – A violent and self-harming inmate in the insane asylum. Obsessed with the Devil.

MISS ADELE NEEDHAM – A confident and flirtatious young American woman travelling on the RMS *Oceanic*. Her sights set on the handsome CAPTAIN SMITH.

MEN

JULES VERNE – World-renowned French novelist. Writer of *Around the World in Eighty Days*. Older man.

HON. WYDHAM CURZON – A young English aristocrat and complete cad. Suave, calculating, arrogant.

THOMAS KETTLE – An Englishman from Birmingham looking for a wife. Defeated by life. Has a permanent cold.

GIOVANNI APOLLONI – The personification of the Italian lover. Outrageous, romantic, full of grand gestures.

RAILWAY PORTER – On New York station.

SAILOR – Takes boat to Blackwell's Island.

DR KINIER – A doctor in the insane asylum. Lacks courage and integrity.

CAPTAIN SMITH – The handsome and upright captain of RMS *Oceanic*. Falls in love with NELLIE.

CHORUSES

CHORUS OF AMERICAN WOMEN – Great supporters of NELLIE BLY who love NELLIE's pioneering spirit.

WOMEN PASSENGERS ON MV *VICTORIA* – A collection of British, French and Italian women. Most of them are young women desperately in search of a husband. Some maiden aunts and widowed mothers.

BRITISH WOMEN IN HONG KONG – The women of the British Empire. Compulsive tea drinkers. Overwhelmingly pleasant, kind, charming and deeply snobbish. Including...

MRS BLATCHFORD-BLAND
MISS DORKING-SNEEZBY
MRS DREADNOUGHT-CUMMING
MISS JONES
A SERVING GIRL

ONLOOKERS AT THE DOCKSIDE – Vicarious thrill seekers.

FEMALE INMATES IN THE INSANE ASYLUM – Some are insane, some are not. Life's casualties. Some see visions, some are dangerous and some are pitiful.

LEPERS – Chinese lepers banished from their homes and communities.

ACT ONE

Prologue

November 1889. **NELLIE BLY**'s *modest apartment in New York.* **NELLIE** *is a tomboyish, confident, perky, self-assured, practical and highly ambitious young woman of twenty-five. She is packing her single bag as she prepares to set off on her solo trip around the world and beat the fictitious eighty days of* **JULES VERNE**'s *hero Phileas Fogg.*

NO. 1: "SEVENTY-FIVE DAYS (OR LESS)"

NELLIE
ONE IDEA, THAT'S ALL IT TAKES A JOURNALISTIC COUP
THEY THINK A WOMAN'S BOUND TO FAIL
WELL MISTER, I'LL SHOW YOU!
IF YOU WANT TO DO IT, YOU CAN DO IT
THE QUESTION IS, DO YOU WANT TO DO IT?
MY ANSWER ALWAYS IS "YES"
IT'S THE SECRET TO MY SUCCESS

SO SEV'NTY-FIVE DAYS I PROMISED THEM
SEV'NTY-FIVE DAYS – OR LESS
WHAT WAS I THINKING IN THAT MOMENT?
NO WONDER MY EDITOR SAID YES
I, NELLIE BLY, WOULD RACE ROUND THE WORLD
IN SEV'NTY-FIVE DAYS, OR LESS

SO HERE I AM, IT'S TIME TO PACK
ONE BAG IS KEY
FOR AFTER ALL THE ONLY THING THAT I NEED IS ME
BUT I'LL TAKE A COAT, THIS TOUGH TWO-PIECE WAS
    DESIGNED TO LAST THE TRIP

A CAP, THREE VEILS, MY SLIPPERS, REST MY FEET WHILST ON THE SHIP
A SMALL INK STAND, PAPER, PENCILS, PENS, SOME NEEDLES AND SOME THREAD
I'VE GOT TO BE PREPARED EN ROUTE, I NEED TO THINK AHEAD
A DRESSING GOWN, A BLAZER, EXTRA UNDERWEAR, SOME SOAP.
A FLASK, A CUP, SOME MONEY WITH THESE THINGS TO HAND I'LL COPE
BUT WAIT THERE'S ONE THING MISSING, THINK! THE CLIMATE I WILL FACE
I NEED TO TAKE MY COLD CREAM, AN ESSENTIAL ON THIS RACE
IF I'M GOING TO GET AROUND THE WORLD IN SEV'NTY-FIVE DAYS, OR LESS

As **NELLIE** *struggles to force the large jar of cold cream into her bag a* **CHORUS OF AMERICAN WOMEN** *appear. They are great supporters of* **NELLIE**. *The* **AMERICAN WOMEN** *can see and hear* **NELLIE** *but she is completely unaware of them.*

WOMEN
OH MY, OH MY, NELLIE BLY
THE ALL-AMERICAN WOMAN
ALWAYS SEEKING OUT THE TRUTH TO GET HER STORY
LEADING THE WAY, TO FEMININE GLORY
OH MY, OH MY NELLIE BLY
HEROINE OF THE USA
AHEAD OF HER DAY, WHILE WE WATCH AND PRAY FOR HER
THREE CHEERS FOR NELLIE BLY

ACT ONE, PROLOGUE

SOLOIST 1	WOMEN
WE LIVE THROUGH HER VICARIOUSLY	AH
SOLOIST 2	**WOMEN**
AS SHE EXPLORES PRECARIOUSLY	AH
SOLOISTS 1 and 2	**WOMEN**
THE WORLD WE YEARN TO	AH

WOMEN and SOLOISTS
>SEE

WOMEN
>SHE'S JUST SO BRAVE
>SHE KNOWS NO FEAR
>A TRUE AMERICAN PIONEER
>OH MY, NELLIE BLY

NELLIE
>NELLIE BLY SO FEARLESS YET BENEATH THE PEN VENEER
>LIZZIE I AM HEARING NOW HER DOUBTS ARE ALL TOO CLEAR
>IS THIS CHALLENGE JUST TOO BIG FOR ME?
>A WOMAN ON HER OWN?

>SHOULD I SEEK A MALE COMPANION?
>DO I NEED A CHAPERONE?
>HOW DO I WALK AWAY WHEN THE ADVENTURE'S BEEN DECLARED?
>I'M TRAPPED BY MY AMBITION
>IT'S IRRELEVANT I'M SCARED

>JUST CLOSE THE BAG AND SHUT THE DOOR, AND PRAY THAT I'LL RETURN
>GOODBYE TO DOUBT
>HELLO TO FOGG
>IT'S TIME TO CHALLENGE MONSIEUR VERNE

Sound effects: Ship's horn blows.

1ST AMERICAN WOMAN Thursday November 14th, 1889.

2ND AMERICAN WOMAN Thirty seconds after 9:40 pm.

NELLIE *takes out her notebook and writes.*

NELLIE *(speaking as she writes)* It's only a matter of 28,000 miles, and seventy-five days and four hours until I shall be back in New York again! *(beat)* What's there to worry about?

NELLIE *picks up her bag and exits.*

WOMEN
OH MY NELLIE, OH MY NELLIE BLY
WITH OUR HOPES AND DREAMS
WE BID YOU GOODBYE
UNCLE SAM HAS NOW BEEN MATCHED
AN ALL-AMERICAN GAL DESPATCHED
EXCITEMENT RISING HERE AT THE DOCK AS NELLIE RACES
 AGAINST THE CLOCK

ONE FINAL WAVE, SHE'S OFF
GOD BLESS
WE'LL SEE YOU HERE IN SEV'NTY-FIVE DAYS
SEV'NTY-FIVE DAYS
OR LESS

Prologue segues to Scene One.

Scene One

Sound effects: Howling storm at sea.

The middle of the night, 15 November 1889. **NELLIE***'s cabin on the MV* Augusta *crossing the Atlantic Ocean. A fierce storm is raging.* **NELLIE** *is desperately seasick and lies groaning with her head in a bowl as the ship pitches and rolls.*

NO. 2: "NEW WOMAN"

NELLIE
OH... OH...
OH... OH...

WHEN WORKING OUT MY VARIABLES
I MISSED OUT EBB AND FLOW
I'M ONLY ON DAY TWO AND THE SEA MAKES ME WANT TO,
GONNA THROW UP

NELLIE and WOMEN
OH...
OH...

NELLIE	**WOMEN**
I'D WORKED OUT THE LOGISTICS	AH
ONE BAG, ONE ME, BOTH TICK	AH
I FAILED TO TAKE INTO ACCOUNT	AH
THAT I GOT TRAVEL SICK	AH
OH NO	NO, NO, NO, NO, NO, NO, NO

NELLIE
IF I FACE EIGHT DAYS OF TORTURE
PLEASE GOD END MY LIFE TONIGHT
THE NAUSEA'S OVERWHELMING, WAVES WITHIN,

NELLIE	WOMEN
OUTSIDE PLIGHT	AH, AH

The **GIBSON GIRL** *dances into the cabin. She is supremely confident, wealthy and beautiful. She is the epitome of the contemporary idea of American femininity. A convention throughout is that only* **NELLIE** *can see, speak to or hear the* **GIBSON GIRL**.

GIBSON GIRL Don't mind me. You go right ahead, Nellie.

> **NELLIE** *vomits. The* **GIBSON GIRL** *inspects the cabin and* **NELLIE***'s belongings.*

NELLIE What are you doing…in my cabin? Who the hell…are you?

GIBSON GIRL Who the hell am I? Nellie, honey, you know very well who I am. I'm the girl every young American woman would like to be. *(beat)* Poor, deluded souls. They can only dream. *(opening* **NELLIE***'s bag)* Goodness, Nellie Bly! Is this all the wardrobe you've brought with you for a solo trip around the world? What if you're invited to a tennis party in gay Paree or a fancy dress ball in Shanghai? What if you were to meet an eligible English lord or a smouldering Russian prince? You'll have nothing whatsoever to wear!

NELLIE I'm aiming to get round the world in seventy-five days. I won't have time for tennis parties or fancy dress balls let alone English lords or smouldering Russian princes… *(groans)* Who the hell are you?

GIBSON GIRL

> I'M THE AMERICAN DREAM
> NEW WOMAN
> CUTE AND FUNNY AND SMART
> GIRLS ADORE ME, THE MEN IMPLORE ME
> (AND THAT'S JUST FOR A START)
>
> YES I'M THE ENVY OF ALL
> NEW WOMAN
> INDEPENDENT AND FREE

ACT ONE, SCENE ONE   7

    IN PROPORTION, APPROACH WITH CAUTION
    MY ONE AGENDA IS ME

    OUT FOR BIKE RIDES IN CENTRAL PARK
    SPORTY, YOUNG AND FIT

    I SWIM, PLAY GOLF, PLAY TENNIS TOO
    SEE THE CONFIDENCE I EMIT
    LET'S DANCE

NELLIE
    OH...
    PLEASE...
    STOP...

GIBSON GIRL
    WE HAVE IT ALL IN EIGHTEEN EIGHTY-NINE
    AN INDEPENDENT LIFE IS MINE
    I CAN DO WHAT I WANT
    I CAN SAY WHAT I THINK

    OH MY DEAR NELLIE, GET BACK TO THE SINK

NELLIE	**WOMEN**
THIS ISN'T THE WAY THAT I THOUGHT THE TRIP WOULD GO	OH WAY, OH GO
I'M ONLY ON DAY TWO AND THE SEA JUST MAKES ME THROW	OH TWO, SEA, THROW
UP	UP
OH...	OH...

GIBSON GIRL
    I'M HERE TO SUPPORT
    TO GIVE YOU A CHEER
    JUDGING BY YOUR CURRENT STATE YOU NEED IT, DEAR

NELLIE
WHAT I FAILED TO REALISE
WAS I GOT TRAVEL SICK

WOMEN
OH, SICK, OH

OH NO

GIBSON GIRL
I'VE HEARD YOUR TRAUMA BUT I'M DONE, DEAR
LIGHTEN UP, WE'VE JUST BEGUN HERE
IT'S THE AGE WHERE WE CAN HAVE IT ALL
AND TOGETHER WE COULD HAVE A BALL

BOTH
EIGHTEEN EIGHTY-NINE, NEW WOMEN
ARE WE

NELLIE
BLEUGH...

NELLIE *(astounded)* You're the Gibson Girl...

GIBSON GIRL You got it! I'm the Gibson Girl. The ideal of the thoroughly irresistible modern American woman. The whole world simply adores me...and who can blame them!

The ship pitches and rolls. **NELLIE** *groans.*

Mal de mer, honey. Eat a cold chicken salad and drink two glasses of pink champagne. Never fails!

NELLIE But you're not a real person... The Gibson Girl is a cartoon character in *Scribner's Magazine.*

GIBSON GIRL I beg your pardon?

NELLIE You're fictitious...made up...a caricature created by Charles Dana Gibson...his vision of the perfect modern American girl.

GIBSON GIRL I know. Aren't I something else!

NELLIE *(to herself)* I'm hallucinating you. This damned seasickness is making me hallucinate. If I close my eyes and count to ten this mirage will have disappeared. *(closes* *her eyes and puts her hands over her ears)* One, two, three, four...

GIBSON GIRL No peeking.

NELLIE ...Five, six, seven, eight, nine...

>   NELLIE *opens her eyes. The* GIBSON GIRL *is still there.* NELLIE *groans.*

GIBSON GIRL Alternatively break two raw eggs into a glass of cognac, add five drops of Angostura bitters and a good dash of cayenne sauce. Kill or cure.

>   NELLIE *retches.*

NELLIE You're not real. Go away.

GIBSON GIRL Nellie, you're a fine one to talk about people not being real. Your real name isn't Nellie Bly! And now here you are bouncing about in the middle of the Atlantic Ocean trying to better Mr Jules Verne's entirely fictitious character Phileas Fogg and his eighty-day journey around the globe. *(She looks around the cabin)* Not the most auspicious of beginnings to your great adventure, is it?

NELLIE Why am I hallucinating you?

>   *The ship pitches.* NELLIE *groans.*

GIBSON GIRL My best guess, Nellie, is because you need me.

NELLIE Fiddlesticks!

GIBSON GIRL You might appear super-confident and fearless but we all know that's only superficial, don't we?

NELLIE Do we?

GIBSON GIRL America's first and foremost female journalist. Intrepid reporter for the *New York World*. *(beat)* The girl who's afraid of nothing and nobody!

NELLIE That's me.

GIBSON GIRL No. That's who you'd like to be.

NELLIE I don't need you!

GIBSON GIRL The girl who'll do anything and go anywhere for a story. Even getting herself committed to an insane asylum for the sake of a scoop.

NELLIE *Ten Days in a Mad House* ...I wrote that book after I got myself locked up in that terrible place in order to expose its cruelties... Thousands of people read my book...tens of thousands. It caused a grand jury investigation. Because of my pioneering journalism, conditions in mental asylums improved! My greatest stunt. Until now that is. *(beat)* When I have gone around the world in seventy-five days or less I'll record all my experiences in another best-selling book! *(The* **GIBSON GIRL** *applauds* **NELLIE***.)* Go away! I don't need anyone to hold my hand!

GIBSON GIRL Tell the truth, Nellie. You're not quite what you appear to be.

NELLIE You know nothing about me.

GIBSON GIRL Oh, Nellie, don't you understand? I'm here to help you.

NELLIE When this ship stops plunging and my seasickness abates then you will disappear like the mist in the morning.

Ship pitches. **NELLIE** *groans.*

GIBSON GIRL You've been trying to become someone else ever since the day you were born Elizabeth Jane Cochrane in that little out-of-the-way nowhere place...what's its called again?

NELLIE Cochran's Mills!

GIBSON GIRL Back in '64.

NELLIE '66. I was born in 1866.

GIBSON GIRL Nellie...stop fibbing. We both know you were born in '64 and that makes you twenty-five years old, not twenty-three as you keep telling everyone.

ACT ONE, SCENE ONE

The ship rolls and pitches. **NELLIE** *groans.*

Eat a concoction of ginger, tamarind and crème de menthe. Guaranteed to have you back on your feet in a matter of moments.

NELLIE *vomits. The* **GIBSON GIRL** *examines* **NELLIE***'s bag.*

Nellie? I'm sure that even the fictitious Mr. Fogg took more than one little bag with him.

NELLIE I'm a working woman! I'll go anywhere...do anything for a great story!

GIBSON GIRL I believe there are some very handsome and eligible young men on this ship.

NELLIE I don't care about handsome and eligible young men... all I care about is getting my story! *(beat)* Go away!

GIBSON GIRL Cochran's Mills, Pennsylvania, July 19th, 1871! Remember?

NO. 3: "YANKEE DOODLE DANDY" - A Cappella, sung by a child's voice offstage

CHILD *(offstage)*
YANKEE DOODLE WENT TO TOWN
A-RIDING ON A PONY
HE STUCK A FEATHER IN HIS HAT
AND CALLED IT MACARONI

GIBSON GIRL Recognise that voice?

NELLIE *(amazed and full of wonder)* Catherine?

GIBSON GIRL That's right, your dear little sister Catherine from way back when... Remember?

NELLIE *(frightened)* No...please no...

GIBSON GIRL Don't be such a baby, Nellie. There's some things you can't forget.

Scene One segues to Scene Two.

Scene Two

Flashback to NELLIE's *birthplace in* COCHRAN's *Mills, Pennsylvania, July 19th 1871.* NELLIE *is seven years old, her sister* CATHERINE *is six.* CATHERINE *comes marching in pretending to be a soldier and singing loudly as she beats a toy drum.*

CATHERINE
YANKEE DOODLE, KEEP IT UP
YANKEE DOODLE DANDY
MIND THE MUSIC AND THE STEP
AND WITH THE GIRLS BE HANDY!

Come on, Lizzie...join in...we're marchin' to Georgia!

GIBSON GIRL You heard your sister, Lizzie. Join in.

NELLIE I'm not Lizzie Cochran anymore. I'm Nellie Bly now...

CATHERINE Hurry up, Lizzie...

GIBSON GIRL Hurry up, Lizzie...

NELLIE *hesitates and then joins* CATHERINE *in her Marching Song.* NELLIE *becomes a seven-year-old again.*

CATHERINE and NELLIE/LIZZIE
FATHER AND I WENT DOWN TO CAMP
ALONG WITH CAPTAIN GOODING
AND THERE WE SAW THE MEN AND BOYS
AS THICK AS HASTY PUDDING

YANKEE DOODLE, KEEP IT UP
YANKEE DOODLE DANDY
MIND THE MUSIC AND THE STEP
AND WITH THE GIRLS BE HANDY!

The two GIRLS *shriek with laughter. Their mother,* MARY JANE COCHRAN *enters.* MRS COCHRAN *is deeply upset.*

NELLIE/LIZZIE Whatever's wrong, mother?

MRS COCHRAN You poor, innocent little mites.

CATHERINE Mother?

NELLIE/LIZZIE Why are you crying, Mother?

   MRS COCHRAN *embraces her two daughters.*

MRS COCHRAN Your daddy's gone away.

CATHERINE Has he gone to Philadelphia, Mother? Will he bring me back a present?

NELLIE/LIZZIE *(to* **CATHERINE***)* No, he's gone to Pittsburg, silly.

MRS COCHRAN Your daddy's passed on. *(The* **CHILDREN** *do not understand).* He's gone to a better place. *(The* **CHILDREN** *still do not understand).* Your daddy has died, my darlings. Gone to live with the angels up in heaven above.

NO. 4: "AN ANGEL ON YOUR SHOULDER"

*(***CATHERINE** *sobs and hugs her mother who comforts, her)* I know, sweetheart, I know...

NELLIE *walks away to stand by herself. The heartbroken and sobbing* **AMERICAN WOMEN** *appear.* **NELLIE**, **CATHERINE** *and* **MRS COCHRAN** *do not see them.*

WOMEN
   A FAMILY IN MOURNING
   TEARS POOL UPON THE GROUND
   THREE LIVES HAVE CHANGED FOR EVER
   THE SENSE OF LOSS PROFOUND

   HEAVEN GAINED AN ANGEL
   BUT THREE HEARTS WERE TORN IN TWO
   HOW BEST CAN WE SUPPORT THEM
   THERE, SO MUCH THEY'LL NEEED TO DO

SOLOIST
THOSE TEARS WILL DRY, THE
GRIEF WILL STAIN
ONLY TIME AND SPACE CAN
DIMINISH PAIN

WOMEN
AH

DIMINISH PAIN

WOMEN
> LORD PROTECT THESE CHILDREN
> IN YOUR CARE THEY NEED TO STAY
> GIVE THEM STRENGTH TO DEAL WITH ALL THE HURT
> THEY FEEL TODAY

NELLIE/LIZZIE Don't cry, Mother. We'll be all right. When I'm older I'll get a job and earn all the money we need.

MRS COCHRAN Don't be thinking thoughts like that, child. *(opening her arms)* Come here.

NELLIE/LIZZIE I'll look after us all, Mother.

MRS COCHRAN Now is not the time for such thoughts, Lizzie.

NELLIE/LIZZIE I'll do it, Mother. *(beat)* Once I've made up my mind I always do what I say I will.

WOMEN
> PRACTICALITIES INTRUDE
> BUT BILLS WON'T WAIT FOR GRIEF
> THE GIRLS ARE RIGHT TO MENTION IT
> HEAR NELLIE'S SELF-BELIEF
> A FAMILY IN TROUBLE
> SHE KNOWS WHAT SHE MUST DO
> LIZZIE'S SLOWLY FADING AS YOUNG NELLIE COMES IN VIEW

NELLIE
> PAPA, PLEASE FORGIVE ME
> FOR THIS PAIN IS ALL TOO RAW
> I'LL MOURN YOUR PASSING LATER NOW MY STRENGTH
> IS NEEDED MORE
> TODAY YOUR DAUGHTER GREW UP
> TO A WORLD TIL NOW UNKNOWN
> A SOB FOREVER PRESENT
> YET THE SILENT CRY'S MY OWN

ACT ONE, SCENE TWO

WOMEN
OH MY, OH MY NELLIE BLY,
CHILD INTO WOMAN IN ONE DAY
TEARS OVER FLOW
BUT NO ROOM FOR HER TO SHOW HER PAIN
NO TEARS FOR NELLIE BLY

The **AMERICAN WOMEN** *disappear.*

Sound effects: The sound of a steam train coming to a hissing stop.

GIBSON GIRL Hate to interrupt such a tender family moment but the famous novelist Mr Jules Verne and his charming wife are waiting on the platform to greet you.

NELLIE What?

GIBSON GIRL We're in France, Nellie... Amiens... 23rd of November...nine days gone...

NELLIE I can't leave them...

GIBSON GIRL *(beat)* Not a moment to waste...schedule's tight.

MUSIC 4 up.

MRS COCHRAN
TRUE TO YOUR WORD THE DAY YOUR FATHER DIED
MY DARLING LIZZIE HAS ALWAYS TRIED
TO PROTECT THIS FAMILY

MRS COCHRAN and **CATHERINE**
BUT NOW WE SAY TO YOU
ON THIS JOURNEY
YOU BE CAREFUL TOO

CATHERINE
RISKS ARE MANY AND CAN'T BE IGNORED
BUT YOU AND AN EXTRA SPECIAL THING ON BOARD

MRS COCHRAN AND CATHERINE
YOU HAVE AN ANGEL ACTING AS YOUR GUIDE

PAPA WILL BE WITH YOU
HE WILL NEVER LEAVE YOUR SIDE

MRS COCHRAN *and* **CATHERINE** *fade back into* **NELLIE**'s *past.*

NELLIE All I ever wanted was for you to be proud of me, Mother.

MRS COCHRAN and **CATHERINE**
YANKEE DOODLE, KEEP IT UP
YANKEE DOODLE DANDY
MIND THE MUSIC AND THE STEP
AND WITH THE GIRLS BE HANDY!

MRS COCHRAN *and* **CATHERINE** *are gone.* ***MUSIC 4*** *out.*

GIBSON GIRL Put on your best face, Nellie…here comes the great Jules Verne and his wife…

Scene segues to a platform on Amiens Railway Station, France.

Scene Three

NELLIE *is effusively welcomed by the limping sixty-one-year-old* **JULES VERNE** *and his wife,* **HONORINE**. *A cold and exact* **FEMALE INTERPRETER** *accompanies the* **VERNES**. *The* **AMERICAN WOMEN** *appear again and sing as the* **VERNES** *greet* **NELLIE**.

NO. 5: "UNCHARTERED WATERS"

WOMEN
>THE TENSION'S STARTED NOW YOU'VE CROSSED THE SEA
>UNCHARTERED WATERS
>DIFFERENT SIGHTS YOU'LL SEE
>WE MUST REMIND YOU THAT YOU'RE IN A RACE
>TO SECURE YOUR GLORY YOU MUST KEEP APACE
>
>WITH THAT IN MIND WE'RE QUITE ALARMED TO READ
>YOU'VE GONE OFF-TRACK WHEN THERE WAS NOT A NEED
>YOU MUST STAY FOCUSED IF YOU WANT TO WIN
>WE NEED YOU TO SUCCEED – YOU ARE OUR HEROINE

SOLOIST 1
>A WARNING TO YOUR EARS THAT YOU SHOULD NOT IGNORE
>SOME TALES ABOUT THE FRENCH THAT WE WERE TOLD
>   BEFORE

WOMEN
>NOW WE SHOULD STRESS THIS IS A RUMOUR
>IT'S JUST WHAT WE'VE HEARD
>THEY'RE ALL CORRUPT, YOU CAN'T TRUST THEM

SOLOIST 2
>(WELL IN TRUTH THAT'S INFERRED)

SOLOIST 3
>THEIR TASTES ARE STRANGE, ALL GARLIC AND SNAILS
>I MEAN HOW DID THAT COME ABOUT

WOMEN
> BE CAREFUL WHAT YOU'RE OFFERED
> AND LEAVE IF IN ANY DOUBT

SOLOIST 4
> OF COURSE THE MEN ARE CHARMING
> THEY THINK ONLY OF ONE THING
> BUT YOU ARE ON A MISSION

WOMEN
> STAY IN FOCUS AND YOU'LL WIN

SOLOIST 5
> THE WOMEN ARE NO BETTER, UNLIKE OUR GOOD HEARTS
> AND TRUE

WOMEN
> BUT THIS IS ALL HEARSAY
> AND WE THOUGHT WE'D PASS TO YOU

The **AMERICAN WOMEN** *exit.*

JULES VERNE *(astonished. To his wife)* Est-ce possible que cet enfant voyage tout seul autour du monde? Mais, mon Dieu, c'est un bébé.

NELLIE I'm sorry... – I don't speak French.

INTERPRETER Monsieur Verne says... Is it possible that this child is travelling around the world alone? Why, she is a mere baby.

NELLIE Please assure Monsieur Verne that I am no baby. I am twenty-three years old.

GIBSON GIRL Oh, Nellie, do stop that fibbing.

NELLIE I'll thank you to stop interrupting.

INTERPRETER *(affronted)* How else am I supposed to do my job?

NELLIE No, not you...sorry...

JULES VERNE Vous pouvez m'appeler *Jules*, mademoiselle.

INTERPRETER You may address Monsieur Verne as Jules.

NELLIE It is a great honour to meet you, Jules.

JULES VERNE Puis-je présenter ma femme, Honorine.

INTERPRETER This is my wife, Honorine.

NELLIE Delighted to make your acquaintance.

HONORINE Moi aussi.

JULES VERNE A votre avis, il faut compter combien de jours pour votre tour du monde ?

INTERPRETER How many days do you think your journey round the world will take?

NELLIE Seventy-five. Perhaps less.

JULES VERNE *(amazed)* Soixante-quinze? Mais, c'est impossible!

The **INTERPRETER** *is about to translate when* **HONORINE** *politely interrupts her.*

HONORINE *(in accented but good British)* My husband believes that it is impossible to make such a journey in seventy-five days.

NELLIE So everyone keeps telling me.

JULES VERNE *(bowing. Kissing* **NELLIE***'s hand)* Enchanté, mademoiselle, et bonne chance.

JULES VERNE *and the* **INTERPRETER** *move away.*

HONORINE *(taking* **NELLIE***'s hand)* I read your book. *Ten Days In a Madhouse.* You are very brave.

NELLIE Or very stupid.

HONORINE I detect a special quality in you, Miss Bly. *(beat)* When I was a young woman of twenty-three...

GIBSON GIRL Twenty-five...she's twenty-five...

NELLIE Shut up!

HONORINE I beg your pardon?

NELLIE Not you... I'm so sorry, you were saying?

HONORINE I had dreams that never came true. If only I'd had the courage to travel around the world by myself...how different my life might have been.

Sound effects: A powerful steam train coming to a halt.

GIBSON GIRL No time to waste, Nellie... Don't miss your train to Brindisi.

NELLIE I must go... It was a great honour to meet you both... *(as she goes)* Au revoir!

HONORINE Au revoir, mon cher!

> **NELLIE** *kisses* **HONORINE** *and hurries away. She pauses, takes out her notebook and begins to hurriedly write.*

NELLIE *(aloud as she writes)* Imagine a youthful face with a spotless complexion...

GIBSON GIRL Hurry!

NELLIE *(aloud as she writes even more hurriedly)* Add to this face pretty red lips, that open to disclose a row of lovely teeth, and large, bewitching black eyes, and you have but a picture of the beauty of Madame Verne... Coming...

> **NO. 6: "CALLING MR RIGHT"** – Intro acts as scene change

> **NELLIE** *and the* **GIBSON GIRL** *hurry off. Scene segues to the promenade deck of the MV* Victoria *crossing the Mediterranean en route from Italy to Egypt.*

Scene Four

A group of highly respectable **WOMEN PASSENGERS** *enter and set up deckchairs and deck games. The* **WOMEN PASSENGERS**, *who are a collection of British, French and Italians, are largely composed of single women desperately searching for a husband. It is a warm day. The sea is calm and the sky is blue. The* **WOMEN PASSENGERS** *start to gossip. The* **GIBSON GIRL** *enters and watches with amusement.*

NO. 6: "CALLING MR RIGHT"

WOMEN
   WHAT A LOVELY DAY TODAY
   CUPID FIRE YOUR DARTS MY WAY
   TIL NOW IT'S ONLY MY LUCK'S BEEN SHOT
   I'M HERE, I'M READY TO TIE THE KNOT
   CALLING MR RIGHT
   LET'S GET THIS SPARK ALIGHT

SOLOIST 1
   MY LAST MAN WENT WITH MY BEST FRIEND
   OF COURSE THAT FRIENDSHIP HAD TO END
   I'VE NOW STOPPED LOOKING FOR A DATE
   INSTEAD I'LL PUT MY TRUST IN FATE

SOLOIST 2
   YOU LOST A FRIEND, YES THAT'S A SHAME
   BUT FRIENDS LIKE MEN YOU CAN REPLACE THE SAME

SOLOIST 3
   MY FIANCÉ, HE CHEATED TOO, BUT WITH MY BROTHER,
      THAT'S REAL PAIN FOR YOU

SOLOIST 4
   A CHEATING MAN YOU COULD RECLAIM
   RED-BLOODED MEN ARE OURS TO TAME
   SO YOU'RE STILL LUCKY NEXT TO ME
   AS MINE DROPPED DEAD WHILST DROPPING TO ONE KNEE

SOLOIST 5
> THE MEN ARE FEW AND FAR BETWEEN
> THE COMPETITION'S STIFF
> MUST STAY SERENE

SOLOIST 6
> BUT I NEED TO WIN, I HAVE HAD ENOUGH
> LIFE UPON THE SHELF IS FAR TOO TOUGH

SOLOIST 7
> I GUESS WE'VE BEEN UNLUCKY UP TO NOW LIFE'S BEEN UNKIND
> HERE'S HOPING ON THIS SHIP A MR RIGHT WE ALL CAN FIND

WOMEN
> A NEEDLE IN A HAYSTACK
> AS THE MEN ARE HARD TO SEE
> REMAINING OPTIMISTIC
> I'LL JUST PRAY THAT THEY'LL CHOOSE ME

> **NELLIE BLY** *steps onto the deck. She does not, at first, see the* **GIBSON GIRL**. *There is an immediate buzz of interest in* **NELLIE** *and gossip about her.* **NELLIE** *takes out her notebook and pencil.*

NELLIE *(aloud as she writes)* "I went out on deck, and the very first glimpse of the lazy-looking passengers in their summer garments, lounging about in comfortable positions or slowly promenading the deck..."

GIBSON GIRL Lovely weather.

NELLIE Goodness! You still here? I thought hallucinations went away.

GIBSON GIRL Must be all that cheese you ate at dinner last night.

NELLIE *(returning to her notebook. Aloud as she writes)* "...standing there alone among strange people, on strange waters, I thought how sweet life is!"

SOLOIST 1
RIGHT DON'T LOOK NOW, THERE'S SOMEONE NEW

SOLOIST 2
HOW BRAZEN

SOLOIST 3
BIG MISTAKE

SOLOIST 4
SHE'S SET HERSELF APART

ALL
A WOMAN ON THE MAKE

SOLOIST 7
NOT A EUROPEAN

SOLOIST 6
LACKS OUR CLASS THAT MUCH IS CLEAR

SOLOIST 7
YET HAS A CERTAIN CONFIDENCE

SOLOIST 2
THAT'S AN AMERICAN VENEER

SOLOIST 3
INTOXICATING PRESENCE

SOLOIST 1
CLEARLY MONIED

SOLOIST 4
STINKING RICH

ALL
WELL THAT'S THE BAIT SHE'LL USE TO GIVE EACH MAN ON BOARD AN ITCH

SOLOIST 3
I FOR ONE DON'T TRUST HER,
WHAT'S SHE WRITING IN THAT BOOK?

ALL
CAN'T YOU GLANCE RIGHT PAST HER

AND TAKE A SNEAKY LOOK?

CURZON *(entering)* Madame...delightful day...nothing like a bracing sea breeze...charmed...

SOLOIST 2
WAIT! NO ONE MOVE
HERE COMES A MAN

ALL
IT'S TIME TO SET ONE'S STALL
OUR CHANCE TO MAKE A MATCH IS NOW
COME LADIES, GIVE YOUR ALL

The **HON. WYNDHAM HENRY CURZON** *enters. The* **WOMEN** *see him.*

SOLOIST 1
PICK ME, I'M CHARMED

SOLOIST 7
HOW I LOVE THE SEA

SOLOIST 1
PLEASE IGNORE THE REST

ALL
WOULD YOU MARRY ME?

CURZON *sees* **NELLIE** *and makes straight for her. The* **WOMEN PASSENGERS** *are jealous and peeved. They are also extremely curious. They strain to hear every word that passes between* **NELLIE** *and* **CURZON**.

CURZON Do I have the pleasure of addressing Miss Nellie Bly?

NELLIE You most certainly do.

CURZON *(kisses* **NELLIE**'s *hand)* Delighted to make your acquaintance, m'dear. I am the Honourable Wyndham Henry Heathcote Roper Curzon, son of the Earl of Egremont, at your service.

The **WOMEN PASSENGERS** *sigh.*

GIBSON GIRL A genuine blue blood, Nellie. Find out if he's got the cash and the castle to go with the title.

NELLIE I don't need any advice from you, thank you.

CURZON I beg your pardon?

NELLIE Nothing... I'm sorry...you were saying?

CURZON I'll come straight to the point, Miss Bly. I find myself in something of a predicament. I am the second son of the Earl of Egremont and for some unaccountable reason my father has decided to disinherit me.

NELLIE How very unfortunate.

CURZON I understand you are an extremely wealthy American heiress. Upon marriage to myself you would immediately be elevated to the ranks of the British aristocracy. All I would require in return would be a modest allowance of one thousand pounds sterling per annum. *(beat)* What do you say?

GIBSON GIRL Slap the bounder's face and send him packing!

NELLIE Are you proposing to me?

CURZON Naturally. I have the lineage and you have wherewithal. *(beat)* We could get spliced soon as we disembark at Port Said.

NELLIE I say...honourable whatever you might be...go get a proper job and leave me alone.

The **GIBSON GIRL** *laughs and applauds.*

CURZON *(affronted)* Really!

As **CURZON** *stalks off the* **WOMEN PASSENGERS** *go into gossip overdrive.*

WOMEN
WHAT JUST HAPPENED THEN, DID YOU SEE?

SOLOIST 2

YES HE WALKED PAST YOU AND YOU, AND ME

SOLOIST 6

WELL HE POPPED THE QUESTION JUST LIKE THAT AND HIM AN ENGLISH ARISTOCRAT

SOLOIST 3

SHE CUT HIM DOWN, AND ANSWERED NO

SOLOIST 6

LACKS CLASS, YOU SEE

SOLOIST 1

I SAY, POOR SHOW

A second man, **THOMAS KETTLE,** *approaches* **NELLIE.** *He is dressed entirely inappropriately for the warm weather and wears a thick, heavy overcoat, a woollen scarf, gloves and a bowler hat. He carries two very large and heavy suitcases. He appears to have a permanent cold and he looks like the weight of the world is on his shoulders. He puts down the heavy suitcases and raises his bowler.*

THOMAS Miss Nellie Bly?

NELLIE The very same.

THOMAS My name is Thomas Kettle and I have been travelling around the world since I was a nipper of nine years old.

NELLIE Fascinating.

GIBSON GIRL Nellie, never ever spend more than thirty seconds in the company of a boring man.

NELLIE I know what I'm doing.

THOMAS *(confused)* I didn't say you didn't.

NELLIE What can I do for you, Mr Kettle?

THOMAS Marry me.

NELLIE *(amused)* And why should I do that, Mr Kettle?

THOMAS Because I have accumulated nineteen large sea trunks on my various voyages and I understand that you travel light.

NELLIE One small piece of hand luggage.

THOMAS Then we are the perfect match.

NELLIE I will not marry you, Mr Kettle. Good afternoon.

THOMAS You are the thirty-eighth young woman to whom I have offered my hand in matrimony. Your rejection therefore comes as no surprise. *(He raises his bowler.)* I wish you a pleasant onward voyage.

As **THOMAS KETTLE** *moves mournfully away the* **WOMEN PASSENGERS** *can hardly contain their excitement and anger. The* **GIBSON GIRL** *is thoroughly amused.*

WOMEN
ANOTHER NO, WHAT IS SHE WAITING FOR?
A KNIGHT ON A WHITE HORSE TO CHARGE RIGHT THROUGH
   THAT DOOR
CLEARLY THE EXCHANGE RATE IS SERVING HER QUITE WELL
TO US THE DOLLAR'S VULGAR BUT THE MEN CAN'T TELL

GIBSON GIRL Oh my, Nellie Bly, aren't you the popular one! *(indicates the other* **WOMEN PASSENGERS***)* But you don't seem to be too big a hit with these ladies.

NELLIE Fiddlesticks to them all! I'm not here to catch a man. I'm a professional working woman doing her job.

GIBSON GIRL Oh, Nellie, have you never felt the stirrings of love?

NELLIE Fiddlesticks to love. I want to work.

1ST FEMALE PASSENGER Would you look at her. Talking to herself now.

2ND FEMALE PASSENGER Too much money combined with a weak mind.

3RD FEMALE PASSENGER Pitiful. Absolutely pitiful.

GIOVANNI APOLLONI *enters. He is the epitome of the romantic Italian lover. All the* **WOMEN** *are entranced and aquiver.* **GIOVANNI** *carries a single red rose.*

4TH FEMALE PASSENGER   (*seeing* **GIOVANNI APOLLONI.** *Overcome*) Oh, mon dieu.

She swoons.

5TH FEMALE PASSENGER   (*unstoppering some smelling salts*) Here...breathe deeply...

The **4TH FEMALE PASSENGER** *revives.*

6TH FEMALE PASSENGER   He's Lord Byron reborn...

7TH FEMALE PASSENGER   He's Adonis!

8TH FEMALE PASSENGER   He's Don Juan!

The **4TH FEMALE PASSENGER** *swoons again.* **GIOVANNI** *opens his arms to* **NELLIE** *and goes down on one elegant knee. He offers* **NELLIE** *the rose.*

GIOVANNI
I NEVER THOUGHT THIS WOULD HAPPEN TO ME
LOVE AT FIRST SIGHT IS AS REAL AS CAN BE
YOU MUST FEEL THE SAME OR MY HEART DIES TONIGHT
HERE'S WHERE TWO BECOMES ONE, AND I JUST HOLD YOU TIGHT

AS YOU LOOK IN MY EYES, YOU SEE STRAIGHT IN MY HEART
AND FROM THIS MOMENT ONWARDS WE NEVER SHALL PART

GIOVANNI *takes* **NELLIE** *in his arms and dances with her.*

WOMEN
SHE'S GOT THE DREAM RIGHT THERE
THAT'S THE MOMENT WE LIVE FOR
BUT SHE DOESN'T CARE
OH WHAT I WOULDN'T GIVE FOR
JUST ONE MOMENT IN THAT FANTASY WHERE I'VE WON THE LOVE PRIZE

WOMEN	GIOVANNI
LOVE AT FIRST SIGHT, WHEN	AH
HE LOOKS IN MY EYES	

GIOVANNI	WOMEN
LET THE MUSIC JUST TAKE	AH
YOU, NO WORDS	
I CAN SENSE WHAT YOU FEEL	AH
THIS IS LOVE, THIS IS REAL	AH

>   NELLIE *disengages herself from* GIOVANNI. *The* GIBSON GIRL *finds it all very amusing.*
>
>   *The music suddenly stops.*

NELLIE That is enough, thank you!

GIOVANNI You are a blessed vision brought to earth by the angels themselves.

>   *The* WOMEN PASSENGERS *all sigh. The* GIBSON GIRL *laughs.*

NELLIE I am a living, breathing woman just like all other living breathing women. *(beat)* And I have the strangest sensation that I've seen you somewhere before?

GIOVANNI I have seen you only in my dreams.

NELLIE You look very familiar… Are you by any chance related to Mr Thomas Kettle or the Honourable Wyndham Curzon? Or Jules Verne, come to that?

GIOVANNI Kettle? Curzon? Verne? Are these swines my rivals? *(Drawing a pistol. The* WOMEN PASSENGERS *gasp with ecstasy.)* Where are they? I will kill them!

NELLIE There's no need for that.

>   *Honour satisfied,* GIOVANNI *puts away his pistol.*

GIOVANNI My name is Giovanni Lorenzo Flavio Apolloni. I am a poet and a painter. But no poem or painting could do justice to your dazzling beauty.

The **WOMEN PASSENGERS** *sigh. The* **GIBSON GIRL** *laughs.*

NELLIE What is it you want, Mr Apolloni?

GIBSON GIRL Oh, I think we all know what Mr Baloney here wants.

GIOVANNI We will elope to my villa on the clifftops above Sorento where the dizzying scent of jasmine and sweet bougainvillea mingle in the evening air. Together we will gaze out over the Bay of Naples and I will take your hand, kiss your lips and taste paradise.

The **WOMEN PASSENGERS** *sigh. The* **GIBSON GIRL** *laughs.*

NELLIE Are you proposing to me, Mr Apolloni?

GIOVANNI If such a heavenly mission can be called a proposal then...yes, I am. *(beat)* Be my wife. Be my queen. Be my goddess!

A final great sigh from the **WOMEN PASSENGERS**. *The* **GIBSON GIRL** *laughs.*

NELLIE *(loudly)* I have to tell you, Mr Appoloni... *(then to all the watching* **WOMEN PASSENGERS***)* I have to tell you all that I am not some fabulously wealthy American heiress with more money than brains as everybody on this ship seems to believe. I am a journalist working for the *New York World* and I am in the process of single-handedly girdling the globe in less days than it took Phileas Fogg in Monsieur Jules Verne's famous novel.

GIOVANNI *and the* **WOMEN PASSENGERS** *are shocked.*

GIOVANNI I do not understand.

NELLIE Then let me put it to you bluntly, Mr Apolloni... In my checking account in New York I have precisely seventeen dollars and ninety-one cents.

GIOVANNI *stands, brushes himself off, takes back his red rose, turns and makes a brisk exit.*

WOMEN
I CAN'T BELIEVE WHAT I HEARD
SHE TOOK US ALL FOR FOOLS
PRETENDING SHE WAS WEALTHY GOES AGAINST THE RULES
SO SHE WAS SIMPLY PLAYING, PASSING TIME ONBOARD THIS SHIP
TOYING WITH EMOTIONS ON HER WORLDWIDE TRIP
AND AFTER OUR WARM WELCOME SHE NOW TURNS TO WALK AWAY
THANK GOODNESS WE CAN LIVE WITH OUR OWN CONSCIENCE AS WE SAY

As the sun disappears behind the clouds and the first raindrops fall the **WOMEN PASSENGERS** *hastily pack away their deckchairs and games and books, giving* **NELLIE** *dark looks of disapproval.*

GIBSON GIRL *(as if hearing something)* What was that?

NELLIE I didn't say anything.

GIBSON GIRL Listen, Nellie...listen...

We hear **MRS COCHRAN**'s *voice from far away.*

MRS COCHRAN *(upset. Angry. Offstage)* Oh my God! The shame!

NELLIE *(alarmed)* Mother?

GIBSON GIRL Better go see what she wants.

NELLIE *hesitates and then rushes off followed by the* **GIBSON GIRL**. *The* **WOMEN PASSENGERS** *enter all sheltering under umbrellas.*

WOMEN
OH MY, OH MY NELLIE BLY
SELFISH TO THE CORE
DISHONEST, UNTRUE
WON'T SPARE A THOUGHT FOR YOU
OH MY NELLIE BLY

Scene Five

Scene segues to the **MRS COCHRAN**'s *small apartment in Pittsburgh, 1884.* **MRS COCHRAN** *is reading a letter* **NELLIE** *has written to the* Pittsburgh Dispatch. **NELLIE** *enters. The* **GIBSON GIRL** *watches.*

GIBSON GIRL So this is when it all began.

NELLIE If you mean my journalistic career then, yes, this is where it all began. *(beat)* Why have you brought me back here?

GIBSON GIRL You'll see.

> **MRS COCHRAN** *suddenly cries out and flings down the letter.*

NELLIE *(stepping into* **MRS COCHRAN**'s *world)* Whatever is the matter, Mother?

MRS COCHRAN I'll tell you what the matter is, my girl! *(brandishing* **NELLIE**'s *letter)* What on God's good earth compelled you to write this shaming diatribe? You will turn the Cochrans into a laughing stock! We will become social pariahs!

NELLIE It's 1884, Mother. Women are no longer the slaves and vassals they used to be. Men no longer tell us what to do, what to think and what to say. We have a voice of our own and that voice must be heard.

GIBSON GIRL *(applauding. Sarcastically)* Bravo! Very good! You could become the first woman President of the United States of America!

NELLIE Do shut up!

MRS COCHRAN I will have my say...

NELLIE Not you, Mother...

MRS COCHRAN To think that a child of mine could write such... profanity! I'm ashamed, Lizzie. Deeply ashamed.

NELLIE It is not you who should be ashamed of me, Mother. It is the editor of the *Pittsburgh Dispatch* who should be ashamed of allowing such misogynistic drivel to be printed in his newspaper. I merely sought to redress the balance.

MRS COCHRAN You've already sent this atrocious letter to the newspaper?

NELLIE Of course.

GIBSON GIRL Always the impulsive one.

NELLIE Be quiet!

MRS COCHRAN I've already told you... I will not be quiet!

NELLIE Not you...

MRS COCHRAN You must withdraw this balderdash immediately!

NELLIE Too late, Mother. Anyways, it's not up to me. It's the editor's decision as to what balderdash he chooses to print.

    CATHERINE *enters. She is nineteen years old.*

CATHERINE What's our Lizzie gone and done now? Robbed a bank? Spit in the eye of the Governor of Pennsylvania?

NELLIE I am no longer Elizabeth Jane Cochran. From now on I wish to be known as Nellie Bly. Like that girl in that song.

MRS COCHRAN You call yourself after a character in a Vaudeville song? The shame!

NELLIE Nellie Bly is my journalistic nom de plume. The name under which I will make my fame and fortune.

MRS COCHRAN You're breaking your poor mother's heart, Lizzie.

NELLIE Nellie.

CATHERINE *(taking the letter from her mother)* Let's see what she wrote?

MRS COCHRAN *(handing* **CATHERINE NELLIE***'s letter)* Your sister has sent this to the *Pittsburgh Dispatch*...

NELLIE It's balderdash, apparently...

MRS COCHRAN It's worse than balderdash...it's heresy!

CATHERINE *(reading* **NELLIE***'s letter and laughing)* Oh, Lizzie... you're wicked!

NELLIE *(incensed)* Two days ago the *Pittsburgh Dispatch* printed a letter from an anonymous father asking for advice about what he might do with five unmarried daughters...

MRS COCHRAN You'll see me to an early grave, Lizzie Cochran...

NELLIE Nellie Bly...

GIBSON GIRL *(giving* **NELLIE** *the relevant edition of the* Pittsburgh Dispatch*)* You'll need this.

NELLIE Thank you...

MRS COCHRAN *(confused)* What for?

NELLIE Listen...this is what one of the *Dispatch*'s esteemed columnists, a certain woman-hater named Erasmus Wilson, wrote in reply to that father's letter... *(She reads from the newspaper.)* "Working women are a monstrosity". "The only place for the fairer sex is in the home" ... "We should take a page out of China's book and consider female-specific infanticide to deal with our excess of girls."

MRS COCHRAN He was joking about the China thing.

NELLIE Joking! If he considers such a statement a joke then I most definitely do not!

CATHERINE You should have been born a boy.

NELLIE I'm very happy being a girl, thank you so much, Catherine. A new kind of girl who's not afraid to stand up for herself and all womankind.

CATHERINE Hallelujah!

NELLIE I have decided I will become a journalist and my reply to Mr Wilson's appalling blather will be my very first article.

CATHERINE Thought you were going to be a teacher.

NELLIE Fiddlesticks to teaching. Writing is my métier.

CATHERINE Your what?

NELLIE Doesn't matter.

CATHERINE *(reading)* "The Girl Puzzle".

NELLIE Good title, don't you think?

MRS COCHRAN I do not!

CATHERINE *(reading)* "What shall we do with the girls?" *(Beat)* "How many wealthy and great men could be pointed out who started in the depths but where are the many women? Let a youth start as errand boy and he will work his way up until he is top of the firm. Girls are just as smart, a great deal quicker to learn; why, then, can they not do the same?"

NO. 7: "THE TIME IS NOW"

Lights snap up on the **AMERICAN WOMEN**. *They are now strident and outraged in support of* **NELLIE**.

WOMEN
 THE TIME IS NOW
 THE PLACE IS HERE
 STAND UP AND MAKE YOUR VOICES COUNT
 WE PERSEVERE
 NELLIE IS RIGHT
 WHAT'S THE BLOCK? WHY THE WALL?
 OPPORTUNITIES SHOULD BE AFFORDED TO ALL

Lights snap out on the **AMERICAN WOMEN**.

MRS COCHRAN I feel faint.

CATHERINE Shall I fetch you a glass of water, Mother?

MRS COCHRAN No thank you, my dear. *(beat)* If your sister continues in these wilful ways I fear it will not be water I will be drinking, but a beverage that is considerably stronger.

NELLIE You're making a great deal of fuss about nothing, Mother.

MRS COCHRAN Nothing? *(Beat. To* **CATHERINE***)* Read out the conclusion of her letter.

CATHERINE "Here would be a good field for believers in women's rights. Let them forego their lecturing and writing and go to work; more work and less talk. Take some girls that have the ability, procure for them situations, start them on their way, and by so doing accomplish more than by years of talking."

Lights snap up on the **AMERICAN WOMEN**.

WOMEN
SUCCINCT AND REALLY CLEAR
NELLIE MAKES OUR POINT
WE'RE STANDING RIGHT BEHIND YOU
OUR LEADER WE ANOINT

MUSIC 7 under.

GIBSON GIRL If there's a drum to beat, you'll beat it until it breaks. But I have to admit...I admire your pluck.

NELLIE Why, thank you kindly.

MRS COCHRAN Why do you keep saying "thank you"?

CATHERINE No man is going to publish this rant.

NELLIE Too late! It's appearing in tomorrow's newspaper!

MRS COCHRAN Lord preserve us!

NELLIE And they've offered me a full-time job...as a journalist! A woman journalist!

WOMEN
IF ONLY WE HAD YOUR COURAGE
IF ONLY WE HAD YOUR NERVE
BUT WE DON'T SO WE STAND BESIDE YOU

WE LISTEN AND OBSERVE
THE WORLD IS CHANGING
THE DIFFERENCE IS YOU
WE GIVE SUPPORT FOR EVERYTHING THAT YOU DO
SO TODAY WE HERE DECRY
HOW WE LOVE YOU NELLIE BLY

NELLIE (*suddenly unsure of herself*) Maybe Mother was right.

MRS COCHRAN Of course Mother is right.

NELLIE Maybe I should have become a teacher, got married, settled down, had a family.

GIBSON GIRL Be brave, Nellie. Stand by your words.

NELLIE I don't know.

MRS COCHRAN Whatever's wrong with the girl?

CATHERINE Lizzie?

GIBSON GIRL Be strong, Nellie. Be strong.

NELLIE (*self-confidence returning*) I will become a crusading female journalist. I will do deeds that men dare not contemplate.

The **GIBSON GIRL** *applauds.*

MRS COCHRAN Catherine...I need to lie down in a dark room.

CATHERINE (*as she helps* **MRS COCHRAN** *to her feet*) Lean on me, Mother.

MRS COCHRAN *and* **CATHERINE** *start to exit.*

MRS COCHRAN Be careful, Lizzie. Be careful of what you dare.

MRS COCHRAN *and* **CATHERINE** *exit.*

GIBSON GIRL You won't be needing that heavy coat here.

NELLIE (*calling*) Mother... I never meant to hurt you...

GIBSON GIRL She's gone. Too late.

NELLIE Where are we?

GIBSON GIRL British Hong Kong, silly! Nellie Bly, I do believe you've made it halfway round the world!

NELLIE Am I still on schedule?

GIBSON GIRL On the money, honey!

Music segues to very proper British tea dance. Instrumental.

Scene Six

Scene segues to a tea dance in a very British corner of Hong Kong. It is hot and humid. A group of refined, upper-class **BRITISH LADIES** *enter carrying parasols. They are extremely polite and proper: the backbone of the British Empire. All hold dainty cups of tea.*

NELLIE *and the* **GIBSON GIRL** *enter. All the upper-class* **BRITISH LADIES** *observe* **NELLIE** *with polite curiosity.* **NELLIE** *immediately takes out her notebook and pencil and hurriedly writes.*

NELLIE *(aloud as she writes)* "We first saw the city of Hong Kong in the early morning. Gleaming white were the castle-like homes on the tall mountainside."

BRITISH LADIES *take a sip of tea.*

BRITISH LADIES *(demurely)* Ah.

GIBSON GIRL Oh my golly gosh! The outpost of empire.

MRS ANSTRUTHER *(approaching* **NELLIE***)* Delighted to make your acquaintance, Miss Bly. We've heard so much about you and your wonderful adventure.

NELLIE Likewise. Miss...Mrs...

MRS ANSTRUTHER My name is Mrs Arthur Anstruther. My husband is second assistant deputy regional undersecretary to the clerk of works to the Governor of Hong Kong. Allow me to introduce Miss Fordham-Buller.

MISS FORDHAM-BULLER How nice to meet an American. And you speak English as well. Will you be staying long in Hong Kong?

NELLIE Not long in Hong Kong.

MRS ANSTRUTHER Mrs Beatrice Murry-McMurray. *(confidentially)* Her husband's in tea.

NELLIE Oh.

ACT ONE, SCENE SIX   41

MRS MURRAY-McMURRAY Am I correct in understanding you are a journalist?

NELLIE That'll be me.

MRS MURRAY-McMURRAY A female journalist. Well I never. Do you write about recipes and wallpaper?

NELLIE No. I write about things that matter.

MRS MURRAY-McMURRAY Ah, a fashion journalist.

MRS ANSTRUTHER Miss Felicity Selhurst-Winner.

NELLIE How do you do?

MISS SELHURST-WINNER Charmed. Absolutely charmed.

MRS ANSTRUTHER Mrs Blower-Blower-Fitzroy.

MRS BLOWER-BLOWER-FITZROY How nice to meet you. Is your husband accompanying you?

NELLIE I don't have a husband.

MRS BLOWER-BLOWER-FITZROY How unfortunate.

GIBSON GIRL Enjoying yourself?

NELLIE You still here?

GIBSON GIRL You need me.

NELLIE I need you to get out of here!

MRS BLOWER-BLOWER-FITZROY *(confused)* I'm sorry?

NELLIE I was talking to myself.

MRS BLOWER-BLOWER-FITZROY It's the heat. Happens to the best of us from time to time.

MRS ANSTRUTHER Lady Ponsonby-Breedlove-Godalming, wife of Major General Sir Ponsonby-Breedlove-Godalming VC, DSO, KCB.

LADY PONSONBY-BREEDLOVE-GODALMING *(brusque)* D'you ride?

NELLIE No...

LADY PONSONBY-BREEDLOVE-GODALMING Shame.

MRS ANSTRUTHER Miss Whickerton-Snickerton.

MISS WHICKERTON-SNICKERTON Play bridge?

NELLIE No.

MISS WHICKERTON-SNICKERTON Never mind.

MRS ANSTRUTHER *(introducing the other* **BRITISH LADIES***)* Mrs Blatchford-Bland... Miss Dorking-Sneezby... Mrs Dreadnought-Cumming and Miss Jones. *(A serving girl hovers.)* Assam or China? Cucumber sandwich? Potted shrimps?

NELLIE No thank you... I'm fine.

MRS ANSTRUTHER *(passing* **NELLIE** *a cup of tea and a sandwich)* Nothing like a spot of tiffin to revive the spirits on a tropical afternoon.

GIBSON GIRL I'd prefer a dry Martini.

NELLIE Would you be quiet!

The **BRITISH LADIES** *look askance.* **NELLIE** *is flustered.*

No, I didn't mean you... I was talking to... *(beat)* ...It doesn't matter.

As **NELLIE** *drinks her tea and nibbles her sandwich the* **BRITISH LADIES** *sing and dance.*

NO. 8: "THE LADIES OF THE COLONY"

ALL
>WE'RE THE LADIES OF THE COLONY
>RUNNING BUSY LIVES STEEPED IN HISTORY
>LIVE BY EMPIRE LAWS IN THE EASTERN SUN
>TEACHING LOCAL FOLK HOW THINGS SHOULD BE DONE

SOLOIST 1
>OUR SERVANTS ALL ARE WONDERS
>WE TREAT THEM AWFULLY WELL

ACT ONE, SCENE SIX

WE NEVER TAKE ADVANTAGE AS WE RING
THE TEA TIME BELL
WE'RE THE LADIES OF THE EMPIRE
AND WE HAVE A ROLE TO PLAY

SOLOIST 2
(OUR HUSBANDS DO THE REAL WORK, WE SUPPORT THEM IN OUR WAY)

SOLOIST 3
BREAKFAST ON THE BALCONY IS HOW I START MY DAY
HUBBY TELLS ME ALL THE NEWS FROM HOME THEN HE GOES ON HIS WAY
THEN I TAKE A STROLL
WE'RE IN HONG KONG, THERE'S LOTS TO SEE

SOLOIST 4
HOW VERY ODD,
HOW STRANGE
HOW QUEER
AS THAT'S THE SAME AS ME

ALL *(giggles)*

SOLOIST 5
NO REST FOR THE WICKED AS BY THEN IT'S TIME FOR LUNCH
CATCH UP WITH THE GIRLS, WE ARE A JOLLY FRIENDLY BUNCH
AND THEN WE GO PLAY BRIDGE, I KNOW
WE REALLY DO NOT STOP
COLONIAL LIFE IS HARD,
WE JUST KEEP GOING TILL WE DROP
THEN HUBBY'S BACK, PLAYS POLO
HE THINKS THE GAME'S TOP NOTCH

ALL
WE DON'T, BUT WE SUPPORT THEM
WE SIT THERE AND WE WATCH

SOLOIST 6
>THEN SUPPER
>MAYBE CRAFTWORK
>WATCH THE SERVANTS AS THEY CLEAN

WOMEN
>THEN IT'S UP AT DAWN TO START AGAIN
>IT'S HOW WE SERVE OUR QUEEN

>EXHAUSTING

MRS ANSTRUTHER You see we really do live very full and satisfying lives in far-flung outposts of empire.

MISS FORDHAM-BULLER We are all dreadfully hoping that you manage to pip that other gal to the finishing line, Miss Bly.

NELLIE *(not understanding)* Other gal...girl? What other girl?

MISS FORDHAM-BULLER Why, that other female American journalist who is also undertaking a solo journey around the world.

NELLIE *(shocked)* What are you talking about?

MISS WHICKERTON-SNICKERTON Your rival. The girl who is racing you around the world. *(beat)* I say, what fun!

NELLIE Nobody's racing me...

LADY PONSONBY-BREEDLOVE-GODALMING I think you'll find they are. *(beat)* Now what was that other gal's name?

MRS BLOWER-BLOWER-FITZROY Somebody Beesands?

MISS FORDHAM-BULLER Busland? Blislam?

NELLIE Bisland? Elizabeth Bisland from that contemptible little rag *Cosmopolitan*?

MRS ANSTRUTHER Yes, that's the girl. Elizabeth Bisland. Is she a friend of yours?

NELLIE *(panicking)* What the hell is going on? So you're telling me I'm in a race now? Where is this damned Elizabeth Bisland?

ACT ONE, SCENE SIX 45

The **BRITISH LADIES** *are shocked at* **NELLIE**'s *outrage.*

MISS WHICKERTON-SNICKERTON I gather she went in the opposite direction to you.

MRS BLOWER-BLOWER-FITZROY And according to this morning's *Hong Kong Telegraph* she is now well in the lead.

MISS WHICKERTON-SNICKERTON She left here three days ago.

MRS ANSTRUTHER Charming girl with perfect manners. Encyclopaedic knowledge of wallpaper.

MISS JONES She told us that she has the authority from her newspaper to pay any amount of money to get ships to leave in advance of their scheduled times.

MISS FORDHAM-BULLER Unfortunately your ship...

MISS JONES The RMS *Oceanic*...

MISS FORDHAM-BULLER Won't be able to leave Hong Kong for another five days.

NELLIE Five days!

MRS BLOWER-BLOWER-FITZROY I'm afraid there's nothing to be done.

NELLIE Jesus wept!

LADY PONSONBY-BREEDLOVE-GODALMING Really, Miss Bly! Standards!

NELLIE This is crazy! Why didn't my newspaper wire me! Am I supposed to kick my heels here in Hong Kong for the next five days while Elizabeth damned Bisland extends her damned lead!

Awkward silence.

MISS FORDHAM-BULLER The Hong Kong Light Operatic and Dramatic Society will be giving a performance of *Ali Baba and the Forty Thieves* at Government House this evening. It promises to be frightfully amusing.

Sound effects: A polite clock strikes five.

MRS ANSTRUTHER *(to* **NELLIE***)* More tea, Miss Bly?

NO. 9: "LADIES OF THE COLONY" – Reprise

BRITISH LADIES
>WE'RE THE LADIES OF THE COLONY
>WE WILL LIFT YOUR SPIRITS WAIT AND SEE
>YOU'VE FIVE DAYS YOU SAY?
>WELL THERE'S LOTS TO DO
>PLEASE STAY WITH US
>OH NELLIE, DO
>
>WE COULD TEACH YOU BRIDGE
>SHOW YOU EVERY SIGHT
>JOIN THE AMATEUR DRAMATICS
>TRY IT OUT TONIGHT
>MAYBE AFTER ALL THAT FUN YOU CHOOSE TO STAY
>
>BECOME AN HONORARY EMPIRE LADY FROM THE U.S.A?
>WHAT FUN!

The **BRITISH LADIES** *leave, wishing* **NELLIE** *good luck.*

NELLIE *(to the* **GIBSON GIRL***)* Why didn't you tell me about this Elizabeth Bisland? Why didn't you tell me I was in a race?

GIBSON GIRL Because I'm a figment of your damned imagination. Remember?

Lights up on **ELIZABETH BISLAND** *on a railway platform. She is waiting for her train. A railway porter stands beside* **ELIZABETH** *with several large trunks on a trolley.* **ELIZABETH** *is elegant, softly-spoken and cultured. Very different to* **NELLIE***.*

NO. 10: "NEW CHAPTER"

ELIZABETH
>FASHION, FABRICS, INTERIOR DESIGN
>THAT'S WHAT I WRITE ABOUT

ACT ONE, SCENE SIX

    THAT'S WHAT I CARE ABOUT
    THAT'S MY CAREER, TO DATE

    SO WHY AM I STANDING AT ANOTHER PLATFORM
    WAITING FOR ANOTHER TRAIN?

GUARD
    WHAT'S THAT? I DON'T KNOW MISS
    BUT IT DON'T SEEM RIGHT I REALLY THINK YOU SHOULD COMPLAIN

ELIZABETH
    I'VE ALWAYS WRITTEN FROM MY HEART
    WRITTEN OF MY PASSION
    ONLY KNOW OF FASHION
    TIME TO MAKE A BRAND-NEW START

GUARD
    SEE IT AS EXCITING
    WOULD THAT HELP YOUR WRITING?

ELIZABETH
    WHY DID I SAY YES TO A RACE I DON'T BELIEVE IN?
    ANYBODY'S GUESS
    I DON'T CARE IF I LOSE OR WIN
    THIS IS NOT THE WRITER I CHOSE TO BE

GUARD
    THEY'RE BAITING YOU TO FIGHT HER,
    OR CAN'T YOU SEE?

ELIZABETH
    TWO WOMEN RACING AROUND THE WORLD
    TO SEE HOW QUICK THEY CAN BE
    AND REGRETFULLY, ONE OF THOSE LADIES IS ME

    Some of the **AMERICAN WOMEN** *appear.*

WOMEN
    WELL THIS WAS UNEXPECTED TWO GLOBE TROTTERS IN A RACE
    WE FEEL WE SHOULD STAY NEUTRAL AS WE WATCH THEM IN THEIR CHASE

AS BOTH OF THEM ARE WINNERS
PROVING WOMEN ARE AS
STRONG AS ANY MAN WHO FIGHTS US
WELL THIS SURELY PROVES THEM WRONG

WE CHEER THEM FROM THE SIDE LINES
KNOWING NEITHER ONE CAN LOSE
A GLORIOUS SITUATION OVER WHICH WE NOW ENTHUSE

Lights up on **NELLIE BLY** *and the* **GIBSON GIRL**.

NELLIE

THIS WASN'T THE WAY IT WAS SUPPOSED TO GO
I'D PULL OFF THIS GREAT STUNT
CREATE THE GREATEST SHOW
THE ONLY PERSON TO BEAT WAS ME
BUT SUDDENLY I'VE HIT A NEW REALITY
NOW SHE'S IN THE LEAD I CANNOT FIGHT BACK
THERE'S NO WAY TO GET MY PLAN BACK ON TRACK
MY RESERVES WERE LIMITED
WHILST HERS WERE VAST
SHE'S WHIZZING ROUND THE WORLD, I CAN JUST GO FAST
WHAT A WASTE OF TIME
SO SHE'S GOT ME BEAT

GIBSON GIRL

JUST LIKE THAT YOU ROLL OVER AND ADMIT DEFEAT
BUT YOU'RE NELLIE BLY
AND YOU DON'T GIVE IN
SO THINGS GOT HARD
BUT YOU STILL COULD WIN

YES SHE'S HAD SOME LUCK
AND SHE'S FINANCED WELL
BUT SHE DOESN'T WANT IT, OR SO THEY TELL
YOU ARE TRAVELLING LIGHT THAT WILL GIVE YOU SPEED

NELLIE

YES I'D HEARD SHE'D PACKED THE KITCHEN SINK

GIBSON GIRL
INDEED!

NELLIE
RIGHT I'M BACK JUST A MINOR BLIP
COMPETITION HELPS TO STEER THE MIND
MY RACE IS STILL THE SAME ONE
THOUGHTS OF QUITTING NOW WELL BEHIND
YES I, NELLIE BLY, WILL RACE ROUND THE WORLD
IN SEV'NTY-FIVE DAYS ... OR LESS

CAPTAIN SMITH *of the RMS* Oceanic *enters. He is young and handsome with impeccable manners.*

CAPTAIN SMITH Miss Bly?

NELLIE Why, yes.

CAPTAIN SMITH I am Captain Henry Smith of the RMS *Oceanic*.

I believe I am to have the pleasure of your company on our voyage to Yokohama and then on to San Francisco. (**NELLIE** *starts to chuckle.*) Is something wrong, Miss Bly?

NELLIE Forgive me, Captain. You are rather different to what I imagined you would be.

CAPTAIN SMITH And how did you imagine I would be, Miss Bly?

NELLIE An old sea dog with short legs and a grey beard and brass buttons straining to hold back his ample stomach.

CAPTAIN SMITH *(smiling)* And I was told that you were an old maid with a dreadful temper. Tell you the truth I was hoping you would miss our ship.

They both laugh.

Allow me to take your bag, Miss Bly.

NELLIE That is most gallant of you, Captain.

GIBSON GIRL Thought you weren't interested in romance.

NELLIE Fiddlesticks!

CAPTAIN SMITH I beg your pardon.

NELLIE Nothing, Captain.

CAPTAIN SMITH This way, Miss Bly.

NELLIE *(hesitating)* You look oddly familiar, Captain. Have we met before?

CAPTAIN SMITH I think not, Miss Bly.

NELLIE You don't have any Italian cousins?

CAPTAIN SMITH No, Miss Bly. None at all.

ALL
OH MY, NELLIE BLY
ANOTHER CHAPTER'S JUST ABOUT TO START
WE'RE GRATEFUL THAT YOU HAD A CHANGE OF HEART
OUR HEROINE DEFYING FEAR,
WE WATCH AND PRAY THEN GIVE A CHEER
WE'RE WITH YOU NELLIE BLY

End of Act One

ACT TWO

Scene Seven

NO. 11: "DON'T LET THEM OUT"

Christmas Day 1889. Sunshine. A warm day. A hillside full of flowers outside Canton, China. The **GIBSON GIRL** *is wearing an elegant and fashionable summer outfit.* **NELLIE** *enters wearing her plaid coat and clutching her bag.*

GIBSON GIRL Oh Nellie, the mercury's practically exploding in the glass and here are you all dressed up for a New York winter. *(She pirouettes.)* D'you like my outfit? The very latest. À la mode.

NELLIE Fashion is not my concern. I'll leave all that to Elizabeth Bisland.

GIBSON GIRL Canton, Nellie. How's it feel to be in proper China?

NELLIE It feels wonderful. Can't tell you how glad I am to have put those ever-so-nice, tea-swilling, cucumber-sandwich-eating, double-barrelled Britishers behind me.

GIBSON GIRL You and Captain Smith seem to be hitting it off.

NELLIE I don't know what you mean.

GIBSON GIRL I'm sure you do, Nellie.

NELLIE *(hastily changing the subject)* Feels like I can see the whole world from this hillside. The whole world and everyone in it.

GIBSON GIRL You can... Look...there's Elizabeth Bisland!

A disgruntled and unhappy **ELIZABETH BISLAND** *appears.* **NELLIE** *and the* **GIBSON GIRL** *watch her.*

NELLIE Is she ahead of me? Is she winning?

ELIZABETH
TWO WOMEN RACING AROUND THE WORLD
TO SEE HOW QUICK THEY CAN BE
AND REGRETFULLY, ONE OF THOSE LADIES IS ME.

ELIZABETH BISLAND *disappears.*

GIBSON GIRL And there's your charming Captain Smith, on his poop deck polishing his binnacle!

CAPTAIN SMITH *appears on the bridge of his ship.* **NELLIE** *and the* **GIBSON GIRL** *watch him.*

NELLIE A girl in every port, I expect.

GIBSON GIRL He's only thinking about one girl.

CAPTAIN SMITH
HOW CAN I BE FALLING FOR A LADY I'VE JUST MET?
THIS IS JUST DISILLUSION GONE TOO FAR
YET THERE SHE STANDS ALL ALONE NO DOUBT PLANNING
   HER NEXT VENTURE
MAYBE SHE'D LIKE A CHAPERONE?

OH MY, NELLIE BLY
LOVE HAS CREPT UP ON ME
LEFT ME IN A QUANDARY
BE MINE, NELLIE BLY
I COULD MAKE YOU HAPPY JUST YOU SEE
OF COURSE AT FIRST YOU'D HAVE TO NOTICE ME

CAPTAIN SMITH *disappears.*

NELLIE *(suddenly anxious)* What's happening?

GIBSON GIRL I was thinking about your greatest journalistic triumph... *Ten Days in a Madhouse!*

NELLIE *(frightened)* That was the past... I'm only interested in the future...racing around the world...

GIBSON GIRL Nellie Bly, ace stunt reporter, gets herself committed to the infamous Blackwell's Island Insane Asylum. You sure made the headlines.

The sunny hillside full of flowers melts away.

NELLIE Please...no...

Flashback to October 1887. A dockside in New York City. A dank and foggy day. A small motorboat is tied up at the dock, a seaman stands at the tiller.

GIBSON GIRL Remember, Nellie? New York. October 1887. You'd got yourself committed to the nation's most infamous asylum for the mad.

NELLIE *(frightened)* I don't want to remember!

GIBSON GIRL Why do you do these stunts, Nellie?

NELLIE Because it's my job...exposing the wrongs of this world... doing the impossible...seeking out the truth.

A pitiful and downtrodden group of **INMATES** *enter, all bound for Blackwell's Island. One inmate is so ill she has to be carried by two other women. They are in the charge of* **MISS GRUPE,** *a brutal nurse/warder who carries a truncheon and has a leather briefcase handcuffed to her wrist.* **MISS GRUPE** *constantly chews a wad of tobacco and from time to time spits out tobacco juice. The* **INMATES** *all wear the same threadbare grey uniforms. A few curious* **ONLOOKERS** *watch the proceedings from a distance.*

INMATES
THEY CALL US MAD, DID THE WORLD JUST GO BAD?
WHO'S INSANE? YOU OR I?
SO MUCH TO FEAR, EACH DECISION UNCLEAR
I'M IN PAIN
HEAR MY CRY
WHY WON'T SOMEBODY HELP ME?

WHY WON'T SOMEBODY CARE?
WHAT HAVE I DONE THAT'S SO AWFUL TO OTHERS
YOU'VE LOCKED ME AWAY - PLEASE DO SHARE?

DEMONS INSIDE ME, YOU'RE LOOKING
CAN YOU SEE THEM TOO?
ARE YOU THERE?
DRAGGING ME DOWN
SO I FEEL LIKE I'M DROWNING IN AIR
DO YOU CARE?

UGLY THE TRUTH THAT I'M HIDING
GREAT THAT YOU'VE LOCKED ME AWAY
I'LL BREAK FREE, WHEN I DO
I'LL COME LOOKING FOR YOU
AND YOU KNOW THAT I'LL FIND YOU SOME DAY

MISS GRUPE

NO ONE WANTS TO HEAR YOU
NO ONE HEARS YOUR CRIES
I CAN SEE RIGHT THROUGH YOU AND THOSE DEMON EYES
LOCKED AWAY FOREVER
FREEDOM'S NOW DENIED
I'LL GIVE YOU A THRASHING GET YOU PURIFIED

ONLOOKERS

LOOK AT THE NUTTERS
SEE THEIR EYES ARE CRAZY
THANK GOD THEY'RE CAUGHT AND LOCKED AWAY
SATAN'S INFECTED THEM
THEIR MIND'S ALL HAZY
THROW AWAY THE KEY WE'RE FORCED TO SAY
DON'T LET THEM OUT TODAY

INMATES

BEEN IN THIS HELL FOREVER
AS EACH RIGHT YOU DO DENY
LIVING IS TOO PAINFUL
LET ME DISAPPEAR AND DIE

ACT TWO, SCENE SEVEN 55

The exhausted INMATES *slump to the ground.* MISS GRUPE *takes a list of names from her briefcase. She counts her charges.*

MISS GRUPE *(reading from a document)* Browne? Nellie Browne? Where are you? Identify yourself immediately!

GIBSON GIRL Browne? That what you called yourself?

NELLIE They mustn't know who I really am.

MISS GRUPE *(angrily)* Browne!

NELLIE *(frightened)* Yes.

MISS GRUPE *(aggressive)* Get yourself over here at once, Browne! *(*NELLIE *hesitates.* MISS GRUPE *shouts.)* At once!

NELLIE *goes to* MISS GRUPE. MISS GRUPE *hands her a tattered grey uniform.*

Put this on!

GIBSON GIRL Indignity upon indignity.

NELLIE Look at these poor suffering souls! Somebody has to help them.

GIBSON GIRL But why is that "somebody" always you?

NELLIE Because...because there's nobody else.

MISS GRUPE *(to the curious onlookers)* You see how this one continually talks to herself. A sure sign of congenital, incurable lunacy.

NELLIE I'm not a lunatic...

MISS GRUPE Listen, Browne, if I say you're a lunatic then you are a lunatic. You have been certified a mad woman by the Court of New York...

NELLIE If you say so.

MISS GRUPE *(brandishing the document)* It's all here in this report!

GIBSON GIRL You could have revealed who you really are...you needn't have done this.

NELLIE No!

MISS GRUPE *(reading)* Miss Nellie Browne presented faraway expressions and crazy looks... In court she she ranted and raved...her behaviour was entirely irrational... *(beat)* In black and white, Browne. You are mad. Understood? Mad!

NELLIE *breaks down. One of the* **INMATES** *goes to* **NELLIE**.

Leave her!

The **WOMAN** *stops.* **MISS GRUPE** *addresses all the* **INMATES**.

My name is Miss Grupe and I am your nurse. *(beat)* I warn you all, never to cross me. *(to* **NELLIE***)* Take off that ridiculous coat and put this on at once!

NELLIE May I not wear my own clothes?

MISS GRUPE The insane do not get to wear their own clothes. From now on you will do exactly as you are told and you will be grateful for all that is done for you!

NELLIE *starts to change into the threadbare grey uniform. The onlookers stare at her.* **NELLIE** *is embarrassed.*

NELLIE Please...may I have a little privacy...

MISS GRUPE The insane do not warrant privacy. *(raising her truncheon)* Put it on!

Without a word the other **INMATES** *surround* **NELLIE** *to shield her from the prying eyes.* **NELLIE** *changes into the uniform.*

All of you...into the boat.

The frightened **INMATES** *crowd into the boat. The boat rocks.*

Sit still! Do not rock the boat! Backs straight! Hands on your knees! Eyes dead ahead!

ACT TWO, SCENE SEVEN 57

NELLIE *(standing)* Miss Grupe, these woman are human beings... we are all human beings...

MISS GRUPE I will brook no arguments, Nellie Browne! Sit down or it will be the worse for you!

The GIBSON GIRL *starts to walk away.*

NELLIE *(desperately)* Don't go! I need you!

GIBSON GIRL I'll be waiting for you, Nellie. Waiting on that hillside full of flowers.

NELLIE Please...

The GIBSON GIRL *exits.*

MISS GRUPE Silence!

NELLIE *sits down next to a pale, frightened and frail girl called* TILLIE MAYNARD. NELLIE *takes out her notebook and furiously scribbles. The sick girl is laid on a filthy mattress. The boats heads out into the fog, bound for Blackwell's Island.*

MISS GRUPE What is that you are writing, Browne?

NELLIE *(trying to hide her notebook and pencil)* Nothing...

MISS GRUPE *(grabbing the notebook. She reads aloud.)* "I found my companions seated on a narrow bench. At one end was a bunk in such condition that I had to hold my nose..." *(beat)* Who are you? *(silence)* I said, who are you?

NELLIE I...I do not know.

MISS GRUPE *rips up* NELLIE's *notebook.*

MISS GRUPE From this moment onwards you don't even breathe unless I give you permission. Is that understood? *(silence)* Is that understood?

NELLIE Yes.

MISS GRUPE Row.

NO. 12: "CAN YOU HEAR ME?"

TILLIE
>WHO ARE YOU?
>WHO AM I?
>WHERE ARE WE GOING?
>WHERE ARE YOU TAKING ME?
>
>CAN I SLEEP, WHEN WE'RE THERE?
>I NEED REST, I NEED MY FAMILY
>
>WHY WOULDN'T MY MISTRESS LET ME SLEEP?
>I WORKED DAY AND NIGHT TO EARN MY KEEP
>I ASKED FOR HELP AND SHE'D JUST SHOUT
>THE DAY THAT I COLLAPSED
>SHE THREW ME OUT
>
>I'LL BE OKAY IN A WHILE ONCE I'VE
>RESTED IN BED
>
>THE PURPOSE OF THIS TRIP?
>WHERE ARE WE HEADED?
>
>CAN YOU HEAR ME?
>I'M ASKING WHERE WE'RE GOING?
>WHAT'S THAT LOOK OF DISGUST, THAT YOUR FACE IS
>   SHOWING?
>HEY I'M HERE!
>I'M EXHAUSTED
>CAN'T YOU ANSWER MY PRAYER
>
>WHY ARE PEOPLE LOOKING?
>WHY DOES EVERYONE STARE?
>ALL THE QUESTIONS WITH NO ANSWERS, THEY COULD
>SEND A GIRL MAD
>I'M SO TIRED
>I'M SO LONELY
>NOW YOU'VE MADE ME FEEL SAD
>
>ARE YOU THERE?
>IS ANYBODY THERE?
>ARE YOU THERE?

MISS GRUPE *laughs and then slowly applauds* **TILLIE**.

MISS GRUPE You are as mad as the proverbial March hare, Tillie Maynard. Any more of your crazy singing and I'll have you locked away in a solitary cell with no light, no food and only the rats for company. Now be silent!

TILLIE *(to* **NELLIE***)* Please help me.

> **MISS GRUPE** *goes to* **TILLIE** *and cruelly pulls* **TILLIE***'s hair.* **NELLIE** *holds the sobbing* **TILLIE***.*

NELLIE This poor child needs love and care...not punishment.

MISS GRUPE *(striking out at* **NELLIE***)* I said be silent! Nellie Browne, you will come to regret the day you ever laid your sorry eyes on me.

The boat reaches the bleak shore of Blackwell's Island.

Out!

The **INMATES** *disembark and stand together on the shore. As the* **INMATES** *sing* **NELLIE** *exits.*

INMATES
 NOBODY IS THERE
 NOBODY CARES
 WE ARE NOW FORGOTTEN IN A WORLD THAT DOESN'T CARE
 VOICES IN A WILDERNESS, THAT NOBODY WILL HEAR
 SENT AWAY FROM EVERYONE
 DOES MADNESS DISAPPEAR?

MISS GRUPE Silence!

Move! *(No one moves.)* I said move!

> **MISS GRUPE** *strikes one of* **WOMEN** *with her rope. The* **INMATES** *and* **MISS GRUPE** *exit.*

NO. 12a: "SCENE CHANGE" segues to next scene.

Scene Eight

NO. 13: "YOUR EYES"

Return to Christmas Day 1889. The sunny hillside full of flowers outside Canton, China. The **GIBSON GIRL**, *still in her elegant and fashionable summer outfit, picks some flowers.*

GIBSON GIRL Cheery blossom. Lilies. Yellow roses. Lilac. *(beat)* Spice. Scent. Mystery.
WE LIVE THE AMERICAN DREAM
NEW WOMEN
CAPTAINS OF OUR OWN SHIP
IGNORE DERISION
MAKE BOLD DECISIONS
SEE LIFE AS ONE LONG TRIP

NELLIE *enters wearing her plaid coat and clutching her bag.*
WE NEED TO SEE EVERY ROAD AS A JOURNEY THROUGH FATE
WE DON'T NEED DESTINATIONS AS THEY JUST LIMITATE
  POTENTIAL
SEE OPPORTUNITIES AND EACH ONE EXPLORE
AND ONCE WE'VE EXHAUSTED IT GO SEEK OUT ONE MORE

THE WORLD IS VAST AND YET OUR MIND'S ARE SMALL
IT'S SURPRISING HOW QUICKLY WE CAN BUILD THAT WALL
IN TRUTH EACH DAY'S A FIGHT AND THE OPPONENT HARD
IT FEELS THE DEALER DEALT THEM EVERY WINNING CARD
BUT IF YOU STAND YOUR GROUND
AND YOU FACED YOUR FOE
AS DIFFICULT A TIME YOU'D HAVE YOU BOTH COULD GROW

EACH ONE YOU FACE IS THE SAME, JUST IN A NEW DISGUISE
BUT IF YOU LOOKED REAL CLOSE
YOU'D SEE THEY HAVE YOUR EYES

NELLIE *(still numb and shocked)* I'd forgotten how terrible it was in that asylum. *(beat)* Don't make me go back there again.

GIBSON GIRL I'm not making you go anywhere, Nellie. I'm your hallucination, remember. The mind plays tricks when you spend too much time on your own.

NELLIE What day is it today?

GIBSON GIRL Why it's Christmas Day, Nellie. Christmas Day 1889.

NELLIE Christmas Day. *(beat)* Mother, Catherine and I would just be leaving church about now and heading home for the Christmas feast. *(beat)* Perhaps it's snowing in New York.

GIBSON GIRL Perhaps. *(beat)* Forty-one days gone, Nellie. You going to let Elizabeth Bisland beat you?

NELLIE She's ahead of me… Everyday I lose a little more time… I don't know. *(beat)* Hell, what's the point?

GIBSON GIRL What's the point? Why, getting the story…telling the world…telling the truth…isn't that what you always say?

NELLIE I'd like to fall asleep here on this idyllic Cantonese hillside and dream of…nothing.

GIBSON GIRL You giving up again, Nellie? You quitting?

NELLIE I'm tired of carrying the world on my shoulders.

GIBSON GIRL Is that the famous Nellie Bly, stunt journalist and fearless seeker after the truth speaking? *(beat)* I ask you again, are you going to let that Elizabeth Bisland from that rag *Cosmopolitan* beat you? (**NELLIE** *doesn't answer*) Because if that's your attitude then there's no point in me remaining. Farewell, Nellie Bly.

The **GIBSON GIRL** *starts to exit.*

NELLIE *(frightened)* Don't leave me!

GIBSON GIRL Are you going to let Elizabeth Bisland beat you?

NELLIE It's not that simple!

GIBSON GIRL Yes or no?

Silence. The **GIBSON GIRL** *starts to exit.*

NELLIE No! *(The* **GIBSON GIRL** *stops.)* Hell, no! *(***NELLIE** *starts to regain her self-confidence.)* I'm not going to let some wallpaper writer beat me! No one gets to a great story before Nellie Bly!

GIBSON GIRL That's the spirit.

NELLIE I'll be the first woman to ever go around the world by herself in seventy-five days...or less!

GIBSON GIRL Or less?

NELLIE Why not? Seventy-four days...seventy-three days... seventy-two days even!

The **GIBSON GIRL** *applauds.*

GIBSON GIRL Very good. *(beat)* When do we sail for Japan?

NELLIE At 3pm today...so there's still time to explore some more of this beautiful country.

GIBSON GIRL I'm sure Captain Smith is looking forward to welcoming you on board.

NELLIE Fiddlesticks to Captain Smith!

GIBSON GIRL Oh, Nellie...you don't mean that.

NO. 14: "DON'T TURN AWAY"

The **LEPERS** *enter. Some hobble, some crawl. Their faces are hidden and cowled, their hands and feet wrapped in filthy bandages. Some beg.*

NELLIE *(hears noise)* What's that? My God! Who...what are these creatures?

GIBSON GIRL *(matter-of-factly)* Lepers. *(***NELLIE** *backs off.)* Abandoned by society. Cast out. *(beat)* You going to write about them when you get back home? Not the sort of thing those nice, genteel New Yorkers want to read about when they're taking their morning coffee.

NELLIE Poor forgotten souls. Of course I'll write about them.

MUSIC 14 up.

As the **LEPERS** *sing* **NELLIE** *opens her bag and takes out a notebook and pencil. She writes.*

LEPERS
>PLEASE LADY HELP US
>THANKS FOR STOPPING
>WE KNOW THAT WE LOOK STRANGE
>
>YES NOT A PRETTY SIGHT
>LESIONS ROTTING
>PLEASE LADY SPARE SOME CHANGE

NELLIE *(reads aloud as she writes)* "The lepers are simply ghastly in their misery. There are men, women and children of all ages and conditions... Many are featureless, some are blind, some have lost fingers, others a foot, some a leg, but all were equally dirty, disgusting and miserable."

LEPERS
>DON'T TURN AWAY AS WE BEG FOR OUR LIVES TODAY
>HAVE YOU SOME CHANGE TO SPARE?
>UGLY A TRUTH AS WE CRAWL RIGHT BEFORE YOUR EYES
>ARE WE TOO MUCH TO CARE FOR?

GIBSON GIRL Is that it? Just words on paper. Doesn't count for much, does it?

NELLIE What do you mean?

GIBSON GIRL Actions, Nellie, actions. Go to them.

NELLIE No!

GIBSON GIRL Go to them. Give them money. Give them hope.

NELLIE I can't.

GIBSON GIRL You must. *(beat)* You have to.

LEPERS
>UGLY A TRUTH AS WE CRAWL RIGHT BEFORE YOUR EYES ARE
>WE TOO MUCH TO CARE?

NELLIE *hesitates and then taking coins from her purse she goes to the* **LEPERS**.

NELLIE Here...take it...

GIBSON GIRL Now touch them.

NELLIE *(terrified)* No.

GIBSON GIRL Touch them, Nellie. You cannot catch leprosy from touching. *(beat)* Show them the real Nellie Bly. The brave Nellie Bly. Touch them.

NELLIE *reaches out and touches one of the* **LEPERS**.

LEPERS
DON'T TURN AWAY AS WE BEG FOR OUR LIVES TODAY

NELLIE When I write my book about my journey around the world I will put these lepers in it. I will give them a voice.

GIBSON GIRL You want to be a saint as well?

NELLIE No. Just the best damned journalist who ever dared to pick up a pen.

Sound effects: A ship's horn sounds in the distance.

Mustn't miss the boat.

GIBSON GIRL Plenty of time.

TILLIE *(desperate)* Where are you, Nellie? I need you.

GIBSON GIRL What happened next?

NELLIE What do you mean...what happened next?

TILLIE Nellie!

GIBSON GIRL Blackwell's Island...the insane asylum...

TILLIE Nellie...

GIBSON GIRL She's calling you...

NELLIE I'm not going back there...

TILLIE Nellie...

GIBSON GIRL She needs you.

LEPERS
    PLEASE LADY HELP US
    THANKS FOR STOPPING
    WE KNOW THAT WE LOOK STRANGE
    DON'T TURN AWAY AS WE BEG FOR OUR LIVES TODAY

The **GIBSON GIRL** *and* **NELLIE** *exit. The* **LEPERS** *are gone. The scene segues back to Blackwell's Island.*

Scene Nine

Flashback. Blackwell's Asylum, October 1887. A large hall with a desk and chair for **KINIER**. *In the corner stands an old and worn upright piano.* **KINIER** *and* **MISS McCARTEN**, *a nurse, are flirting. The* **GIBSON GIRL** *watches.*

DR KINIER Even on such a chilly morning as this, the very sight of you, my dear Miss McCarten, is enough to set any red-blooded man's pulse racing.

MISS McCARTEN Why, Doctor, you are so formal this morning. You know very well my name is Aggie.

DR KINIER Were anyone to hear us conversing in such intimate terms...Aggie...they might misinterpret our relationship.

MISS McCARTEN I don't know what you mean, Doctor.

DR KINIER You have the reports on the new inmates?

MISS McCARTEN Right here.

DR KINIER Bring them over to me, would you?

MISS McCARTEN Certainly, Doctor.

MISS McCARTEN takes the reports to the **DOCTOR**. *They stand very close together.*

DR KINIER Miss McCarten, do I detect the scent of rose water?

MISS McCARTEN A girl needs something to take away the stink of this madhouse, Doctor.

DR KINIER Indeed she does. *(moving closer to* **MISS McCARTEN***)* Intoxicating.

MISS GRUPE enters. The **DOCTOR** *and* **MISS McCARTEN** *quickly move apart.*

MISS GRUPE The first batch of new inmates are waiting to be examined.

ACT TWO, SCENE NINE   67

DR KINIER Bring them in...if you must.

MISS GRUPE *(shouts)* Hurry up! Don't keep the doctor waiting.
*(***TILLIE MAYNARD, MARY HUGHES** *and* **NELLIE** *enter.* **TILLIE** *is shaking with the cold. The* **GIBSON GIRL** *also enters and watches the proceedings.)* Stand still! Eyes front!

DR KINIER takes TILLIE's face in his hands and looks into her eyes. He steps back.

DR KINIER Tongue.

TILLIE *hesitates.*

MISS GRUPE You heard the doctor. Tongue!

TILLIE I'm cold. So cold.

MISS GRUPE Tongue!

DR KINIER inspects TILLIE's tongue. He moves to MARY. He looks into her eyes. He steps back. MARY *puts her tongue out. He moves to* NELLIE. *He reaches out to touch her.*

NELLIE *(pulling away)* Don't touch me!

MISS GRUPE Hysterical.

NO. 15: "CLINICALLY INSANE"

MISS McCARTEN The doctor has to touch you, you silly girl, in order to examine you.

DR KINIER Put out your tongue.

Reluctantly **NELLIE** *puts out her tongue.*

NAME?

TILLIE
MY NAME IS TILLIE TILLIE MAYNARD
I AM COLD
I AM FRIGHTENED
AND I WANT TO SLEEP

I THINK SLEEP WOULD HELP ME BEST

HAVE YOU BROUGHT ME HERE TO REST?

DR KINIER
NAME?

MARY
MY NAME IS MARY HUGHES
I'M NOT MAD
WHY AM I HERE?
MY CHILDREN WILL BE MISSING ME
I'M A MOTHER FIRST
WHY CAN'T YOU SEE I'M ALRIGHT
JUST LET ME GO
I JUST MISS MY CHILDREN SO

DR KINIER
NAME?

NELLIE
MY NAME IS NELLIE BROWNE
STATING ON RECORD I AM SANE
I THINK THAT IS PLAIN TO SEE

DR KINIER
AGE?

TILLIE
TWENTY FIVE

MARY
TWENTY SIX

NELLIE
NINETEEN

DR KINIER
DO YOU SEE FACES ON THE WALL?

ALL THREE
WE DON'T SEE FACES ON THE WALL

DR KINIER
DO YOU HEAR VOICES IN YOUR HEAD?

ALL THREE
> WE DON'T HEAR VOICES IN OUR HEAD
>
> THE ONLY SOUNDS THAT WE HEAR ARE THE CRIES AT NIGHT
> WEEPING AND AWAILING OTHER PATIENTS WHO ARE FRIGHTENED
> CRIES FOR HELP
> SOBS OF PAIN
> ONE THEN ANOTHER
> AGAIN AND AGAIN
> HAUNTING THE RESTING STATE OF MIND
> HOW CAN THIS PLACE BE SO UNKIND?
>
> SO NO IS THE ANSWER PUT NICE AND PLAIN

DR KINIER
> I DECLARE ALL THREE
> CLINICALLY INSANE

TILLIE I was told I was going to a convalescent ward…

MISS GRUPE Silence!

DR KINIER No, let her speak.

TILLIE *(breaking down)* I just need to sleep and rest…that's all… I'm cold…if I was warm I would get better… I know I would…

MARY My children will be missing their mother…

NELLIE Can't you see that these women are just as sane as you?

DR KINIER My dear Miss Browne, madness can be a cleverest of all deceivers. Here on Blackwell's Island we know what's best for you. *(beat)* Take them away, Miss Grupe.

MISS McCARTEN And close the door on your way out.

NELLIE Please…

MISS GRUPE Very good, Doctor.

> **MISS GRUPE** *escorts* **NELLIE, TILLIE** *and* **MARY** *out of the consulting room.*

Sound effects: A bell rings loudly.

TILLIE (*frightened*) What was that?

MISS GRUPE Only the breakfast bell, you silly, demented child.

Other INMATES *enter carrying long benches. Some are clearly insane and jabber away to themselves, others are silent and haunted. All are frightened. They sit bolt upright on the benches.* TILLIE *and* MARY *join them.* NELLIE *remains standing.*

If you don't sit you don't eat. If you don't eat you die.

TILLIE I'm cold.

MISS GRUPE Silence!

NELLIE *sits and, like the other* INMATES, *is given a bowl of broth and a spoon.* NELLIE *takes one sip and spits it out.*

Not good enough for your refined tastes, Browne? Soon you'll be so hungry you'll eat any slop that's put in front of you.

The INMATES *bolt down their food.*

SARAH Miss Grupe?

MISS GRUPE What?

SARAH Would you come here, please?

MISS GRUPE This had better be good or you'll be in for it. (*standing in front of* SARAH) What?

SARAH *throws the remains of her bowl of broth into* MISS GRUPE's *face and then shrieks with laughter.* MISS GRUPE *blows a whistle.* MISS McCARTEN *and* DR KINIER *rush in and the three of them seize* SARAH. MISS GRUPE *slaps and beats* SARAH.) Rope Gang!

SARAH Please...

MISS GRUPE Rope Gang! *(*MISS McCARTEN *and* DR KINIER *manhandle the protesting* SARAH *out of the room.)* All of you! Clean this place up!

The bowls and the benches are struck GRUPE *and* INMATES *exit.* NELLIE *and the* GIBSON GIRL *are alone. The asylum melts away and the sun shines.* NELLIE *is back on the hillside in Canton.*

NELLIE Why do you take me back to the past to relive the things I want to forget?

GISBON GIRL *(interrupting the scene)* I'm not taking you anywhere, Nellie. Look, we're still on that hillside in Canton. *(pointing)*

NO. 16: "DROWNING IN AIR"

Over there lies the *Oceanic* at anchor with Captain Smith waiting to greet you. Soon you'll be on your way to Yokohama and then San Francisco and then New York. Home. *(beat)* You can just walk away if you want, Nellie. No one's stopping you.

A light comes up on TILLIE MAYNARD.

TILLIE Don't leave me, Nellie...

Pause.

NELLIE I have to go.

GIBSON GIRL I know.

The sunlit hillside in Canton melts away. Return to the asylum. The INMATES *enter and begin to walk up and down the room. The* GIBSON GIRL *watches.* MISS GRUPE *loses interest in the* INMATES *and chews on her tobacco. As the* INMATES *walk* NELLIE *takes out a crumpled scrap of paper and writes.*

INMATES
WHO? WHAT? HOW?

WHERE AM I?
WHY? COULD? WOULD?
HEAR MY CRY

STOP! WAIT! CALM! PURIFY
SOMEBODY HELP ME I'M DROWNING IN AIR
I'M CALLING FOR HELP AND NOBODY IS THERE

I'M SANE YOU'RE NOT LISTENING
I NEED TO GET OUT
YOU HAVE STOLEN MY WORLD
I AM FULL OF SELF-DOUBT

The **GIBSON GIRL** *takes the scrap of paper from* **NELLIE** *as the* **INMATES** *continue to trudge up and down.*

GIBSON GIRL "...To be a companion, day and night, of senseless, chattering lunatics; to sleep with them, to eat with them, to be considered one of them, was an uncomfortable position..."

INMATES
CAN'T ESCAPE INSANITY
WHEN YOU KNOW YOU'RE SANE
THEY LOCK THE DOOR
DISCARD THE KEY
SOMEBODY PLEASE HEAL MY PAIN

GIBSON GIRL "Compare this with a criminal, who is given every chance to prove his innocence. Who would not rather be a murderer and take the chance for life than be declared insane, without hope of escape?"

TILLIE
HEY! I'M STILL HERE
CAN YOU SEE ME?
I KEEP ASKING FOR HELP
CAN YOU HEAR ME?
I'M EXHAUSTED
SOMEONE ANSWER MY PRAYER
SOMEONE SHOW ME THEY CARE

MARY
MOTHER'S HERE
HAVE NO FEAR
I'LL COME HOME TO MY CHILDREN SO DEAR
DON'T GIVE UP MOTHER'S HERE
HAVE NO FEAR
DON'T GIVE UP TO MY CHILDREN
I LOVE YOU SO

INMATES
WE'RE IN HELL
WE'RE FORGOTTEN
NO MEMORY
OUT OF MIND, OUT OF SIGHT, LEFT BEHIND
NOBODY TO HEAR OUR SAD CRYING
THIS IS CRUEL TO BE KIND

TILLIE	MARY	INMATES
HEY!	MOTHER'S HERE	WE'RE IN HELL
I'M STILL HERE	HAVE NO FEAR	WE'RE FORGOTTEN
CAN YOU SEE ME?	I'LL COME HOME TO MY CHILDREN SO DEAR	NO MEMORY
I KEEP ASKING FOR HELP		OUT OF MIND, OUT OF SIGHT, LEFT BEHIND
CAN YOU HEAR ME?	DON'T GIVE UP MOTHER'S HERE	
I'M EXHAUSTED	HAVE NO FEAR	NOBODY TO HEAR OUR SAD CRYING
SOMEONE ANSWER MY PRAYER	DON'T GIVE UP MY CHILDREN	
SOMEONE SHOW ME THEY CARE	I LOVE YOU SO	THIS IS CRUEL TO BE KIND

ALL
CAN'T ESCAPE INSANITY
WHEN YOU KNOW YOU'RE SANE
THEY LOCK THE DOOR
DISCARD THE KEY
SOMEBODY PLEASE HEAL MY PAIN

TILLIE falls into a fit. She writhes on the floor. NELLIE *starts to go to* TILLIE.

MISS GRUPE Stay where you are!

NELLIE *hesitates.*

Leave her on the floor...it will teach her a lesson.

MISS GRUPE *slaps* TILLIE*'s face until* TILLIE *stops fitting and falls unconscious.* NELLIE *goes to* TILLIE *and holds her and comforts her.*

NELLIE There, there, Tillie...you'll be alright...you'll see...

MISS GRUPE Such compassion, Miss Browne. The very milk of human kindness. *(to the* INMATES*)* Fetch the tub.

Three INMATES *exit to fetch the tub and pitcher of water, scrubbing brushes and a filthy towel.*

Take your clothes off, Browne.

NELLIE I refuse.

MISS GRUPE Very well. *(to the* INMATES*)* Undress her.

Most of the WOMEN *do not move but three or four of the most obviously insane set upon* NELLIE. *They rip off her outer garments.* NELLIE *furiously fights them off.*

Have it your own way, Browne, but tonight you'll be sleeping in wet clothing. *(beat)* Into the tub with her!

NELLIE *is hauled into the tub. The pitcher of freezing cold water is poured over her head. The insane* WOMEN *set about scrubbing* NELLIE *with manic energy.*

That's enough!

The insane WOMEN *step back. Dry her. One of the* INMATES *approaches* NELLIE *with the filthy towel.* NELLIE *flinches with revulsion as the* INMATE *towels her)* Let that be a lesson to you, Nellie Browne. In here *you are nothing but another lost, mad girl. (beat) I'd say it's time for some entertainment. Do you play the piano, Nellie?* **NELLIE** *nods her head. Good. Give us all a tune then. Something to raise the spirits.* **NELLIE** *does not move.*

Play!

Shivering and distressed, **NELLIE** *staggers to the piano. She strikes a note. It is horribly out of tune.*

NELLIE I cannot play this...

MISS GRUPE Play!

NO. 17: "ARE YOU THERE?"

Very tentatively **NELLIE** *starts to play* ***"HOME SWEET HOME"*** *on the out-of-tune piano. One by one the* **INMATES** *join in and sing.*

INMATES
 TO THEE, I'LL RETURN
 OVERBURDENED WITH CARE
 THE HEART'S DEAREST SOLACE
 WILL SMILE ON ME THERE

 NO MORE FROM THAT COTTAGE
 AGAIN I WILL ROAM
 BE IT EVER SO HUMBLE
 THERE'S NO PLACE LIKE HOME

 HOME! HOME!
 SWEET, SWEET HOME!
 THERE'S NO PLACE LIKE HOME

 HOME! HOME!
 SWEET, SWEET, HOME
 THERE'S NO PLACE LIKE HOME
 THERE'S NO PLACE LIKE

 WHO? WHAT? HOW?
 WHERE AM I?

WHY? COULD? WOULD?
HEAR MY CRY

DON'T TURN AWAY AS WE BEG FOR OUR LIVES TODAY
UGLY A TRUTH, WE NEED HELP THERE'S A BETTER WAY

STOP! WAIT! CALM! PURIFY
WON'T SOMEONE HELP ME I'M DROWNING IN AIR
I'M SCREAMING FOR HELP BUT NOBODY'S THERE
ARE YOU THERE?
ARE YOU THERE?
ARE YOU THERE?
DO YOU CARE?

MISS GRUPE *slams down the piano lid on* **NELLIE**'s *fingers.* **NELLIE** *screams.*

The **INMATES** *scatter and exit with* **MISS GRUPE**. *The* **GIBSON GIRL** *and* **NELLIE** *exit.*

Scene Ten

NO. 18: *"RETURNING HOME (INSTRUMENTAL)"*

Sound effects: Sounds of steam-driven liner at sea.

Scene segues to the deck of the RMS Oceanic. *Evening. Moon and stars.*

The RMS Oceanic *crossing the Pacific Ocean heading for San Francisco from Yokohama, Japan.* **CAPTAIN SMITH** *stands staring out to sea.* **MISS ADELE NEEDHAM**, *a young American woman, approaches him. Her intention is to flirt with* **CAPTAIN SMITH**.

MISS ADELE NEEDHAM A penny for your thoughts, Captain.

CAPTAIN SMITH *(startled)* Why, Miss Needham... I was taking the air.

MISS ADELE NEEDHAM Isn't it glorious.

CAPTAIN SMITH It is indeed. *(beat)* If you'll excuse me.

   CAPTAIN SMITH *starts to go.*

MISS ADELE NEEDHAM Captain...we dock tomorrow in San Francisco?

SMITH Yes, we've made record quick time.

MISS ADELE NEEDHAM But I've haven't yet received an invitation to dine at the Captain's table. Tonight's our last opportunity.

CAPTAIN SMITH *(eager to get away)* I'll speak to my steward...

MISS ADELE NEEDHAM I'd feel awfully cheated if I don't get a single chance to have you all to myself over a crab consommé. You're such a popular man, Captain Smith.

CAPTAIN SMITH I'm sure my steward will find a place for you at my table this evening. Good evening, Miss Needham.

MISS ADELE NEEDHAM Adele, please.

CAPTAIN SMITH Good evening, Miss Needham.

MISS ADELE NEEDHAM You're deserting me already?

NELLIE and the GIBSON GIRL enter and watch.

CAPTAIN SMITH I have my duties to attend to.

MISS NEEDHAM I hope you don't regard passing the time of day with me as a 'duty', Captain Smith.

CAPTAIN SMITH Not at all but a ship needs its Captain.

MISS ADELE NEEDHAM takes CAPTAIN SMITH's arm.

MISS ADELE NEEDHAM Won't you walk with me for a minute or two, Captain? A stroll around the deck. Then you can go back to your silly seafaring duties.

A reluctant CAPTAIN SMITH walks with MISS ADELE NEEDHAM.

GIBSON GIRL Oh my, someone's not backward in coming forward, is she? And with your Captain Smith, as well.

NELLIE He's not my Captain Smith.

GIBSON GIRL I've seen the way he looks at you and the way you look at him.

NELLIE We should reach San Francisco by the December 22nd, if not before. Well ahead of schedule.

GIBSON GIRL He'd be quite a catch.

NELLIE Hop on the express train to New York. By golly, I think I can better seventy-five days.

CAPTAIN SMITH sees NELLIE.

CATAIN SMITH Miss Bly.

GIBSON GIRL Just look at his eyes light up.

NELLIE Everything depends on the progress of that damned Elizabeth Bisland!

GIBSON GIRL I wouldn't worry too much about her, if I was you.

ELIZABETH BISLAND *appears. She is frustrated, angry and exhausted. Only the* **GIBSON GIRL** *can see her.*

ELIZABETH BISLAND Curse the day that hussey Nellie Bly dreamed up this damn-fool idea of going around the world on her ownsome! Damn! Damn! And damn her again!

Lights snap out on **ELIZABETH BISLAND**. **NELLIE** *beams.* **CAPTAIN SMITH** *politely breaks away from* **MISS NEEDHAM** *and heads towards* **NELLIE**.

GIBSON GIRL Here he comes. Give him your most dazzling smile!

CAPTAIN SMITH Why, Miss Bly, you look radiant tonight.

NELLIE As do you, Captain Smith.

NO. 19: "TEN DAYS IN A MAD HOUSE"

CAPTAIN SMITH
MISS BLY, I AM DELIGHTED THAT I FINALLY GET TO GREET YOU

NELLIE
CAPTAIN, YOU'RE REALLY RATHER SWEET

CAPTAIN SMITH
RACING ROUND THE WORLD IN UNDER EIGHTY DAYS
IS A BRAVE AND DARING FEAT

NELLIE
LET'S NOT SPEAK TOO SOON, AS I'M NOT HOME
YET, BUT IN YOUR HANDS I FEEL I WILL ACHIEVE
THIS MAMMOTH TASK I SET OUT TO COMPLETE
YES! IN YOUR HANDS I'M STARTING TO BELIEVE

GIBSON GIRL
WELL LISTEN TO THAT, IS THAT FLIRTING I HEAR?

MISS ADELE NEEDHAM
SO HE'S NO TIME FOR ME, BUT HE'S GOT TIME FOR HER?

GIBSON GIRL
> THIS IS MARVELLOUS NEWS, DO I SENSE LOVE IN THE AIR?

MISS ADELE NEEDHAM
> WHAT IS IT ABOUT HER? SHE'S OUT TO ENSNARE

GIBSON GIRL
> IS THIS HAPPINESS CALLING?
> IS YOUR HEART BEATING FAST?

MISS ADELE NEEDHAM
> WHY'S HE WASTING HIS TIME

GIBSON GIRL
> HAS A LOVE SPELL BEEN CAST?

MISS ADELE NEEDHAM
> I AM HURT, I AM BRUISED, I'M NOT AFFORDED A GLANCE

GIBSON GIRL
> THIS COULD BE YOUR LUCKY MOMENT, THIS COULD BE YOUR LAST CHANCE

NELLIE
> YOUR SHIP IS QUITE SPLENDID
> THE BEST THAT I'VE SAILED ON

CAPTAIN SMITH
> MISS BLY, YOU ARE REALLY TOO KIND
> TO TELL YOU THE TRUTH, YOU'RE NOT AT ALL WHAT I EXPECTED – QUITE THE LADY. CLEARLY REFINED.

NELLIE
> WHY CAPTAIN, I'M BLUSHING
> YOU'VE CAUGHT ME OFF GUARD THERE
> YOUR SENTIMENT AND WORDS ARE REALLY BOLD

CAPTAIN SMITH
> WELL I THOUGHT THAT A LADY AS FEARLESS AS YOU, MISS, COULD HANDLE SOME HOME TRUTHS JUST BEING TOLD

GIBSON GIRL
> IT'S MOVING SO QUICKLY, SHE'S LOSING CONTROL

MISS ADELE NEEDHAM
>CAN'T WATCH ANY LONGER, IT'S TAKEN IT'S TOLL

MISS ADELE NEEDHAM *storms off.*

GIBSON GIRL
>DEAR NELLIE, YOU'VE EARNED THIS
>MAKE ROOM IN YOUR HEART
>JUST STAY OPEN AND WARM SO A ROMANCE CAN START

CAPTAIN SMITH
>PLEASE DON'T THINK ME PRESUMPTUOUS
>BUT I'M TAKING THIS CHANCE
>WE'RE ALL ALONE ON THIS DECK
>AND I HEAR MUSIC
>LET'S DANCE

>**NELLIE** *and* **CAPTAIN SMITH** *dance break.*

>YOUR ADVENTURE'S NEARLY OVER
>NEW YORK IS IN SIGHT
>WOULD YOU DO ME THE HONOUR OF DINNER ONE NIGHT

NELLIE
>OH CAPTAIN, MY CAPTAIN
>WHAT A LOVELY IDEA
>BUT MY LIFE IS TOO BUSY FOR DINNER, MY DEAR.

>**CAPTAIN SMITH** *leaves dejected.* **NELLIE** *wipes some tears away.*

GIBSON GIRL
>WHAT IS WRONG WITH YOU
>WHY DID YOU TAKE THAT FALL
>YOU JUST HAD A CHANCE
>TO HAVE IT ALL

NELLIE
>NO THE TIMING'S WRONG
>I STILL HAVE A JOB TO DO
>I NEED TIME ALONE
>I NEED TIME AWAY FROM

The **INMATES** *from the asylum enter with* **MISS GRUPE.** *She chews tobacco. The* **INMATES** *sing.*

INMATES
   WHO?

NELLIE No, I can't go back there. Stop them...no, NO!

INMATES
   WHAT

MISS GRUPE Where have you been, Nellie Browne?

NELLIE Miss Grupe, I am not insane. I wish to go home.

INMATES
   HOW?

MISS GRUPE Did you hear that ladies? Poor Nellie Browne wants to go home. You're going nowhere. Walk.

INMATES
   WHERE?

Scene Eleven

The **INMATES** *trudge up and down the hall. The* **GIBSON GIRL** *watches.*

INMATES
WHO? WHAT? HOW?
CAN'T YOU SEE?
WHY? COULD? WOULD?
HEAR MY PLEA

STOP! WAIT! CALM
PURGATORY

SOMEBODY HELP ME I'M DROWNING IN AIR
I'M CALLING FOR HELP AND NOBODY IS THERE
I'M SANE YOU'RE NOT LIST'NING
I NEED TO GET OUT

YOU HAVE STOLEN MY WORLD I AM PLAGUED WITH SELF-DOUBT

CRAZY

CLARA
DAMNED FOR ETERNITY

ANNA
DREAMED OF MY MOTHER LAST NIGHT
THINK SHE MAY COME TODAY AND TAKE ME HOME

TILLIE
I'M SO COLD
SOMEONE PLEASE HEAR ME

INMATES
LIFE ON THIS MERRY-GO-ROUND
SHACKLED AND HELPLESS AND BOUND
EVERYONE'S LOST TO BE FOUND

AILEEN
HURRAH! THREE CHEERS
I HAVE KILLED THE DEVIL

INMATES
  LUCIFER! LUCIFER! LUCIFER!

  Loud cheers. **AILEEN** *continues to shout, rant and scream.* **MISS GRUPE** *beats her. The* **INMATES** *become very disturbed.* **MISS GRUPE** *wades into them, swinging her truncheon.*

  MISS GRUPE *loses control. Some of the* **INMATES** *turn on her.* **DR KINIER** *enters.*

DR KINIER *(shouts)* What's going on here?

MISS GRUPE I was teaching these demented fools a lesson!

DR KINIER I see. *(beat)* Now, you women...you behave. You hear me? Behave.

  DR KINIER *turns to leave.*

NELLIE Won't you help them? Are you blind? *(beat)* Help them!

  Short silence.

DR KINIER *(shamed)* Carry on, Miss Grupe.

  The **INMATES** *slowly return to their trudging up and down.* **MISS McCARTEN** *enters. Everyone stops walking.*

MISS GRUPE What now?

MISS McCARTEN There's a lawyer from New York come for Nellie Browne.

MISS GRUPE What do you mean?

MISS MCCARTEN The lawyer says she's to be released.

MISS GRUPE She's going nowhere.

MISS McCARTEN The Warden himself instructed me to inform you that you must release Nellie Browne immediately.

MISS GRUPE You heard her, Browne. Get out of here.

ACT TWO, SCENE ELEVEN

> NELLIE *embraces* TILLIE *and some other* INMATES. *It is an emotional parting.*

NELLIE I'm going to expose this place. I'm going to write a book... *Ten Days in a Madhouse.* I'm going to make things better.

MISS GRUPE Get out! Get out!

> *The* WOMEN *resume their trudging up and down.* NELLIE *and the* GIBSON GIRL *watch.* NELLIE *takes out a scrap of paper and writes quickly.*

NELLIE *(aloud as she writes)* "I looked forward so eagerly to leaving the horrible place, yet when my release came and I knew that God's sunlight was to be free for me again, there was a certain pain in leaving. For ten days I had been one of them. Foolishly enough, it seemed intensely selfish to leave them to their sufferings."

> NELLIE *and the* GIBSON GIRL *exit.*

INMATES
CAN'T ESCAPE INSANITY
WHEN YOU KNOW YOU'RE SANE
THEY LOCK THE DOOR
DISCARD THE KEY
SOMEBODY PLEASE HEAL MY PAIN

> *The* INMATES *and* MISS GRUPE *exit.*

NO. 20: *"THE ARRIVAL (INSTRUMENTAL)"*

Scene Twelve

Sound effects: A steam train travelling at speed and the distant sound of cheering.

Scene segues to a compartment in a railway carriage on a train just outside New York City. The GIBSON GIRL *sits waiting for* NELLIE.

GIBSON GIRL *(looking out the window. Calling to* NELLIE, *who is preparing herself)* There's thousands of them out there! Flags, banners... "Welcome Home Nellie Bly" ...why, I do believe you're more famous than President Cleveland...

NELLIE *comes hurrying into the compartment, fussing her hair and doing up her buttons.*

NELLIE How do I look?

GIBSON GIRL Exactly the same as you've looked for your entire journey around the world.

NELLIE *(peering through the window)* Oh, my goodness! All these people, just for me!

GIBSON GIRL Just for you!

NELLIE What's the date?

GIBSON GIRL You know very well what the date is.

NELLIE Just say it.

GIBSON GIRL Saturday January 25th, 1890.

NELLIE Saturday January 25th, 1890! Seventy-two days since I set out on my odyssey! Seventy-two days!

GIBSON GIRL You did it, Nellie.

NELLIE I most certainly damned well did!

GIBSON GIRL And according to the latest reports, Elizabeth Bisland is being tossed about by Atlantic storms and won't reach New York for at least another four days!

Lights up on **ELIZABETH BISLAND** *in her cabin on board a ship in a storm.* **ELIZABETH BISLAND** *groans and then vomits. Lights snap out on her.*

NELLIE Oh, what a terrible shame.

GIBSON GIRL You won.

NELLIE You're damned right... I won!

Sound effects: The steam train comes to a noisy halt. Sound of cheering increases.

GIBSON GIRL Are you ready?

NELLIE As I'll ever be.

NO. 21: "STAR-SPANGLED BANNER (INSTRUMENTAL)"

Lights snap out on the train compartment. Lights up on the railway platform. The **CHORUS OF VERY EXCITED AMERICAN WOMEN** *rush in and deck out the platform with patriotic bunting.*

1ST AMERICAN WOMAN Here she comes!

2ND AMERICAN WOMAN Where are the flowers? Someone get the flowers!

The flowers arrive. Lights up on the door of the train compartment. The door opens and **NELLIE** *steps out.*

The **CHORUS OF VERY EXCITED AMERICAN WOMEN** *rush forward to greet* **NELLIE**.

MUSIC 21 out.

1ST AMERICAN WOMAN Three cheers for our Nellie Bly!

NO. 22: "SEVENTY-FIVE DAYS (OR LESS)" – Finale. Reprise

Hip hip...

AMERICAN WOMEN Hurrah!

1ST AMERICAN WOMAN Hip Hip...

AMERICAN WOMEN Hurrah!

1ST AMERICAN WOMAN Hip Hip...

AMERICAN WOMEN Hurrah!

Sound effects: Cannons from Fort Greene and battery boom out.

NELLIE *is showered with flowers from the cheering crowd.*

NELLIE
ONE IDEA THAT'S ALL IT TAKES
A JOURNALISTIC COUP
THEY THOUGHT A WOMAN WAS BOUND TO FAIL
WELL DIDN'T I SHOW YOU
THAT IF YOU WANT TO DO IT
YOU CAN DO IT
THE QUESTION ALWAYS IS
HOW MUCH YOU WANT TO DO IT

ALL
YOUR ANSWER ALWAYS IS YES
IT'S THE SECRET TO YOUR SUCCESS

SO SEV'NTY-FIVE DAYS YOU PROMISED THEM
SEV'NTY-FIVE DAYS ... OR LESS

PHILEAS FOGG HAS LOST HIS RECORD
AS FOR BISLAND WE CAN ONLY ... GUESS
BUT YOU, NELLIE BLY, RACED AROUND AND YOU
FINISHED IN SEV'NTY-TWO DAYS NO LESS!

MRS CATHERINE COCHRAN
SHE'S A YANKEE DOODLE DANDY
YANKEE DOODLE DO OR DIE

OH MY, OH MY NELLIE BLY
THE ALL-AMERICAN WOMAN

ALWAYS SEEKING OUT THE TRUTH TO GET HER STORY
LEADING THE WAY TO FEMININE GLORY
OH MY! OH MY NELLIE BLY
HEROINE OF THE USA
AHEAD OF HER DAY
WHILE WE WATCH ON AND PRAY FOR HER
WE LOVES YOU NELLIE

Suddenly **MUSIC 22** *cuts dead.*

As **MUSIC 22** *cuts dead all action freezes except for* **NELLIE**. *It is as if she is suspended in time.*

NELLIE *(to the* **GIBSON GIRL**, *who* **NELLIE** *supposes is standing behind her)* Would you look at all these people...the flowers...the flags...what a welcome... I can't believe my eyes...

NELLIE *becomes aware that the* **GIBSON GIRL** *is no longer at her side.*

Come out here... It's your moment as well... *(beat)* ...Where are you? *(now becoming concerned that the* **GIBSON GIRL** *is not there)* Where have you gone? You were right by side for the entire... *(***NELLIE** *realises why the* **GIBSON GIRL** *has disappeared. She doesn't need her any more)* Like mist in the morning.

NELLIE *smiles.* **NELLIE** *laughs.*

Thank you! Thank you! Thank you!

TILLIE *enters.*

TILLIE Thank you.

NELLIE Tillie...

TILLIE *embraces* **NELLIE**.

MUSIC 22 *returns.*

The **CHORUS OF VERY EXCITED AMERICAN WOMEN** *come alive.*

ALL
OH MY NELLIE,
OH MY NELLIE BLY
NEVER STANDING STILL
TIL THE NEXT GOODBYE

TILLIE
SO YOU HEARD ME
YOU ANSWERED MY PRAYER
NELLIE BLY, YOU WERE THE
ONE THAT WAS THERE

TILLIE *joins others.*

ALL
SHE'S OFF AGAIN
WHERE? WE JUST CAN'T GUESS
MAYBE WE'LL SEE YOU HERE IN SEV'NTY-FIVE DAYS
SEV'NTY-FIVE DAYS
OR LESS

As **TILLIE** *sings...*

MUSIC 22 *out.*

End

PROPS

ACT ONE

PAGE	ITEM	CHARACTER
1	Single Bag	NELLIE BLY
2	Coat	NELLIE BLY
2	Cap	NELLIE BLY
2	3× veils	NELLIE BLY
2	Slippers	NELLIE BLY
2	Soap	NELLIE BLY
2	Ink stand	NELLIE BLY
2	Paper	NELLIE BLY
2	Pencils	NELLIE BLY
2	Pens	NELLIE BLY
2	Needles and thread	NELLIE BLY
2	Underwear	NELLIE BLY
2	Soap	NELLIE BLY
2	Dressing gown	NELLIE BLY
2	Flask	NELLIE BLY
2	Cup	NELLIE BLY
2	Money	NELLIE BLY
2	Blazer	NELLIE BLY
2	Cold cream	NELLIE BLY
3	Notebook and pen	NELLIE BLY
5	Bowl (for being sick)	NELLIE BLY
12	Toy drum	CATHERINE
21	Deck chairs	BOAT PASSENGERS
21	Deck games	BOAT PASSENGERS
21	Deck books	BOAT PASSENGERS
26	Heavy overcoat	TOM KETTLE
26	Gloves	TOM KETTLE
26	Scarf	TOM KETTLE
26	Bowler hat	TOM KETTLE
26	2× large suitcases	TOM KETTLE
28	Red rose	GIOVANNI
28	Smelling salts	5TH PASSENGER
29	Pistol	GIOVANNI
31	Umbrellas	FEMALE PASSENGER

33	Letter	**MISS COCHRAN**
35	*Pittsburgh Dispatch* newspaper	**GIBSON GIRL**
40	Parasols	**POSH BRITISH**
40	Dainty tea cups	**POSH BRITISH**
42	Cup of tea	**MRS ANSTRUTHER**
42	British sandwiches	**MRS ANSTRUTHER**
46	Several large trunks	**ELIZABETH BISLAND**
46	Trolley	**ELIZABETH BISLAND**

ACT TWO

PAGE	ITEM	CHARACTER
51	Plaid coat	**NELLIE BLY**
53	Small motorboat	**SEAMAN**
53	Truncheon	**MISS GRUPE**
53	Handcuffs	**MISS GRUPE**
53	Leather briefcase	**MISS GRUPE**
53	Chewing tobacco	**MISS GRUPE**
55	List of names	**MISS GRUPE**
55	Tatty uniform	**MISS GRUPE**
57	Filthy mattress	**MOTORBOAT**
59	Rope	**MISS GRUPE**
60	Flowers (cherry blossom, lilies, yellow roses, lilac)	**GIBSON GIRL**
64	Purse with coins	**NELLIE BLY**
66	Piano	**ASYLUM**
66	Desk and chair	**ASYLUM**
70	Long benches	**INMATES**
70	Bowls of broth and spoons	**INMATES**
70	Whistle	**MISS GRUPE**
72	Crumpled scrap of paper and pencil	**NELLIE BLY**
74	Tub and pitcher of water	**INMATES**
74	Scrubbing brushes	**INMATES**
74	Filthy towel	**INMATES**
88	Patriotic bunting	
88	Flowers	**AMERICAN WOMEN**

VISIT THE SAMUEL FRENCH BOOKSHOP AT THE ROYAL COURT THEATRE

Browse plays and theatre books, get expert advice and enjoy a coffee

Samuel French Bookshop
Royal Court Theatre
Sloane Square
London
SW1W 8AS
020 7565 5024

Shop from thousands of titles on our website

- samuelfrench.co.uk
- samuelfrenchltd
- samuel french uk

Lightning Source UK Ltd.
Milton Keynes UK
UKHW022020150419
341049UK00006B/592/P